Sew
Eco

Sew Eco

Sewing Sustainable and Re-Used Materials

Ruth Singer

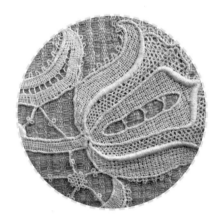

A & C Black • London

Dedication

In memory of my Auntie Ann

First published in Great Britain in 2010
A&C Black Publishers Limited
36 Soho Square
London W1D 3QY
www.acblack.com

ISBN: 978-14081-0284-8

Copyright © 2010 Ruth Singer
Illustrations © Gina Barrett
Photography © Ruth Singer & Sam Eaton

CIP Catalogue records for this book are available from the
British Library and the U.S. Library of Congress.

Typeset in 11 on 14pt Officina Sans

Book design by Susan McIntyre
Cover design by Sutchinda Thompson
Commissioning editor: Susan James

Printed and bound in China

This book is printed on FSC paper.

Mixed Sources
Product group from well-managed
forests and other controlled sources
www.fsc.org Cert no. SGS-COC-003548
© 1996 Forest Stewardship Council
FSC

Contents

Acknowledgements

Many thanks go to Gina Barrett for the illustrations created with skill and patience. I could not have completed this book without a great team of pattern testers; Joan L. Gaddoniex, Ruth MacLure, Amanda Palmer, Anne Redwood, Toni-Ann Riley and Gill Usher. Any remaining mistakes are my own. Immense gratitude to Lisa Harland of Harlands Organic Furnishings for so willingly and cheerfully sharing her expertise on fabrics over the years; to Sarah White for her thorough and thoughtful reading of the draft; to Rachael Lazenby and Kate Unwin for modelling my creations; to my agent Sophie Gorrell Barnes of MBA Literary Agents and finally to my ever-supportive family, particularly Sam Eaton for additional photography.

Introduction

If you already sew, you know just how satisfying it is to select fabric, lay it out, pin, cut, assemble and create. You know how wonderful it is when people admire something you have made, and ask if you will make one for them too. If you don't sew yet, but are thinking about it, let this book inspire you. Sewing is a creative activity, a relaxation, a change from the rest of our busy lives. It's a very contemplative thing to do, particularly hand sewing – settle down with the radio or a DVD to do your hand hemming and enjoy the process. Once you get into the zone of your sewing, time flies, worries are forgotten and wonderful things are created purely by *your* hands. In the last few years, the world has finally caught up with those of us who love to sew. Other people are starting to realise that it's not an eccentric hobby – it's a fun, creative and relaxing thing to do. It's almost become fashionable, especially in financially-straitened times, to make things for yourself rather than buy them on the high street. And sewing has the added benefit of being green. If you don't already sew and are thinking about it, go ahead and try it; if you want to have fun while also being eco and stylish, sewing is the way to go. Reducing our consumption and thinking about the ethical consequences of our shopping habits are positive steps. Mainstream shopping is full of ethical concerns; clothes could be made with child labour, using fabrics treated with chemicals, made from non-renewable resources, shipped round the world then driven across the country before they make their way into our homes. Making our own clothes, cushions, bags and gifts helps break some of this cycle, but much of the fabric from local shops is still likely to be treated with chemicals and produced in less than fairtrade conditions.

A few years ago I started to think about how I could sew eco rather than just sew. There is no reason why sewing eco should be any less stylish than non-eco. In fact it could be more stylish, using vintage fabrics and beautiful natural fibres. It is gradually becoming easier to make green choices in our everyday lives, whatever budget we are on. In our sewing decisions, we can also make moves towards being more green by choosing to recycle, re-use and reduce consumption, or by buying organic fabrics which are produced without polluting chemicals.

The aim of this book is to help you understand the issues involved so you can make your own choices about how you want to 'green' your own sewing. There are so many steps you could possibly take, but no-one can be 100% green. What is super-green for one person might seem feeble to another. It is a matter of learning about the issues, changing what you can, and working towards what the goals you prioritise. I like to think of this as *low-impact* sewing; choosing fabrics that have a lighter environmental load than the average. Choosing to use vintage, recycled and organic fabrics may seem limiting – there are so many lovely non-organic fabrics in the shops that it can be hard to say no to them all. So maybe try 'all things in moderation', start by adding a few vintage fabrics, some basic organic cotton and a couple of pieces of re-vamped old clothing alongside conventional fabrics rather than suddenly going completely fabric-shop cold turkey. Gradually you may come to find that you prefer working with organic fabrics and enjoy the challenge of hunting out vintage fabric and other things to recycle. We will explore shopping for and working with vintage and recycled fabrics; what to buy, how to care for old fabrics, suitable uses for recycled garments and other textiles, and what types of organic and sustainable fabrics are available. In addition, this book will show you how to use recycled materials in place of synthetic interfacing and how to make eco cushion inners instead of polyester ones. If you are learning how to sew, the techniques guide will tell you everything you need to know to complete the projects in this book. The projects themselves are stylish, modern and original and include clothes, fashion accessories and things for your home, for all levels of ability. We have also included some restyling – taking old clothes and accessories and using them to create fabulous new pieces. You can either follow the projects to the letter, or use them to spark off your own designs using the ideas and techniques that follow. Above all, this book is about having fun with fabric while being as eco as possible. Enjoy.

Ruth Singer, 2010.

www.seweco.co.uk

1 Textiles and the environment

Making ethical and environmental choices about textiles is a complex business. This section provides information about the different fabrics available and the issues around textile production. Further information can be found using the Resources section on pp.142-3.

Fabrics

During their production, fabrics are usually treated with chemical finishes and dyes; these have pollution impacts and have also been linked to health problems among farmers. Fabrics may continue to release chemicals when we are wearing them. Legislation and environmental protection has been massively increased in the West in recent years, but other countries still do not have anti-pollution guarantees and systems in place throughout their textile industry.

As well as being a health hazard for workers, chemicals in fabrics have been linked to allergies, particularly related to formaldehyde, which is a suspected carcinogen. It is necessary for soft-furnishing fabrics to be treated with fire-retardants for safety reasons but there are campaigns to increase the use of non-toxic alternatives. See p.16 for more on dyes and finishes. As a general rule, thorough washing of new fabrics will reduce the amount of residual chemicals. Organic fabrics will not have been treated with chemicals during growing or processing.

Cotton

The majority of the worlds' 24 million tonnes of cotton produced annually is grown and processed using hazardous chemicals, scarce water resources, large amounts of (fossil-fuel derived) energy and without sufficient fairtrade regulations to protect the farmers and processors. It has been calculated that a single non-organic T-shirt's worth of cotton would have used 150g of pesticides, often made using petrochemicals and scarce resources. The main areas of cotton production are the US, China and India so the fabric also travels a long way to reach sewing shops in other parts of the world.

Wool

While it is in no way as chemically-intensive as cotton production, wool production can also be environmentally damaging. Of particular concern is the use of pesticides used to treat sheep and to clean wool. If carefully managed and subject to environmental guidelines, the impact of both can be minimised and this makes wool a fairly low-impact fibre. Animal welfare should also be taken into consideration in regard to wool; PETA (People for the Ethical Treatment of Animals) have campaigned for Australian sheep farmers to stop a treatment called 'mulesing' where part of the skin is cut away to prevent infection. Agreements are now in place to find alternative treatments with fewer animal welfare concerns.

Wool fabric is still subject to chemical treatment in the processing and dyeing stages, so even if the fibre itself is fairly low-impact, its production may not be. Wool production is also water-intensive and the effluent created by cleaning raw wool is potentially polluting.

It is worth considering that a lot of woollen fabric for sale in the UK and the US comes from Australia or New Zealand, rather than being made from the wool of local sheep – 24% of the world's wool comes from Australia. Despite the fact that top-quality wool made England rich in the Middle Ages, most sheep now bred in the UK are for meat and their wool is of low quality. Much of it goes to waste, although some is used for carpets.

Hemp

A lot has been written about hemp as the new super-eco wonder fibre. Hemp production requires much less water than the production of other plant fibres, and it is naturally pest-resistant so chemical treatments are not necessary. Hemp grows fast and its land-use is highly efficient compared to other plant fibres. However, it is closely related to cannabis so cultivation is restricted in many countries; this limits its commercial applications. Transforming the plant to fibre does create pollution, but controlled production can limit the impact. Hemp fabric can be as coarse as hessian sacking or as soft as the finest linen - it is extremely versatile. Hemp also grows in Europe so often travels fewer miles than cotton does to the UK market.

Organic hemp

Silk

There is a lot of debate about whether silk can count as a
green fibre or not. As a natural fabric, it is renewable and
biodegradeable and therefore theoretically sustainable. Silk is
made from the threads produced by the silk moth larvae to
make its chrysalis. In commercial production, the silkworms
are killed in the chrysalis to preserve the cocoon intact
before the moth eats its way out. This produces a long,
single filament thread which makes lustrous and strong
fabric. Wild or Tussah silk is produced in a more worm-
friendly way, allowing the moths to live their natural life
cycle. The fibres are therefore short lengths and must be spun
together like wool or cotton, to produce a thread suitable for
weaving; this is usually a natural brown colour rather than the
creamy white of cultivated silk. As the creature isn't killed as part
of the process, this is often called vegetarian or peace silk. Although

Peace silk

production of peace silk may involve limited chemical intervention it isn't
usually certified organic. Some silk producers are working towards chemical-free
silk production and new products should be available in the near future.

Manufactured cellulose-based fabrics

Fabrics such as rayon and viscose, plus newly developed bamboo, soya and
lyocell (brand name Tencel) fabrics are created from natural materials (plant
cellulose such as beech or bamboo) using industrial processes. The plant material
is broken down using solvents before it is processed into a fibre. Viscose requires
significant chemical input during the production phase while the newer fibre,
lyocell, is created using an environmentally-safe process in which the chemicals
are recycled and emissions carefully controlled (called a closed-loop process).
Lyocell is produced in various parts of the world including the US, Europe and
the UK. It has been well received by environmentalists, on the whole, although
some have reservations regarding residual chemicals in the fabric.

Bamboo

Bamboo has also been heralded as a super-eco fibre because it grows quickly and
without much chemical intervention. Like viscose, it requires chemical processing
so some environmentalists have dismissed bamboo as the new eco fabric saviour.
Single-crop agriculture (like soya) has been linked to environmental degradation
and deforestation. Almost all production is in China, so fabric-miles are a major
issue for UK, European and US users and concerns have been raised about the

energy-intensive production process. Like its older cousin, viscose, bamboo fabric is a good alternative to silk in the way it feels and drapes. The next few years will probably see improvements made to bamboo production and processing which may yet make it an ideal eco fabric.

Linen

Linen is a natural fabric, produced from the flax plant. Although it has been cultivated in Europe for hundreds of years, it is now difficult to buy locally-produced linen. Some is produced in the EU but most is from China, former USSR countries and Egypt. As with cotton and other fibres, linen processing uses chemicals, including formaldehyde as a crease-resistant treatment. Organic unbleached or eco-bleached linen is available (see Stockists pp.139).

Organic linen

Ingeo

Ingeo or PLA (polylactic acid polymer) is a new type of fibre developed from a natural resource, in this case maize, similar to other cellulose fibres (see p.13). It isn't yet widely commercially available and the main use of the technology so far has been for biodegradeable plastic bags and packaging. While in many ways it seems a perfect sustainable fabric solution, concerns have been raised about how practically compostable inego is in standard facilities and, like bamboo, how destructive large-scale mono-culture of the source plant material might be.

Hessian

Hessian is made from jute, a plant which is grown commercially in India and Bangladesh. It needs little synthetic fertilizer and few other chemical treatments, so is to some extent an eco fabric and is certainly a sustainable fibre. Hessian is a rough, scratchy fabric commonly used for sacks, but is also used in traditional upholstery and as backing for rag rugs. Organically-produced hessian is not currently available, but the production is believed to be fairly low in chemicals; however, as it is generally used for upholstery, it may be treated with fire retardants.

Leather

In terms of its eco-credentials, leather is just as complex as fabrics. Some will argue that leather is a by-product of the meat industry and is therefore a waste material being efficiently re-used. It is also sustainable and biodegradable, in its natural state. Vegetarians and others might argue that animals should not be farmed so intensively for meat anyway, so by using leather we are encouraging the industry. When considering shoes, the alternatives are often petrochemical-based plastics, which are hardly environmentally impact-free. In terms of home sewing leather is a minor issue, but it is worth knowing that conventional leather is treated with hazardous chemicals in the processing and particularly in dyeing stages. Naturally-tanned or vegetable-tanned leather is a good eco alternative and you may want to investigate small producers who can verify the source of their leather and give you assurances on animal welfare (see Stockists on p.139). I have used recycled and scrap leather and suede in the both the Suede Cushion (p.85) and the Embellised Coat (p.120).

FABRICS AT A GLANCE

Fibre	Sustainable source?	Environmental impact	Alternative
Cotton	Yes	High. Chemicals, intensive agriculture, water use and air miles.	Organic cotton or hemp.
Wool	Yes	Medium-low, if local and sustainably produced. Some chemical use.	Un-dyed, low-impact production or organic.
Silk	Yes	Medium. Silk worms killed, chemicals used in processing. Air miles.	Wild or peace silk.
Cellulose	Yes	Medium. Chemically-processed from natural resource. Tencel is low impact.	Lyocell (Tencel), Ingeo/PLA or bamboo. Hemp. Organic cotton, peace silk.
Hemp	Yes	Low. Local and sustainable, low water and no chemical use. Often organic.	
Bamboo	Yes	Medium. Some arguments against production methods used for bamboo fibre.	
Ingeo/PLA	Yes	Low. Processing is low-impact. Mono-culture of the raw material (maize) is the main concern.	
Synthetics	No	Medium. Made from oil but uses little energy and water to produce.	Organic or sustainable fabrics.

Dyes and other fabric treatments

Fabrics undergo a number of treatments which we, as buyers, may not be aware of. Even natural fibres like cotton or wool may have been treated with chemicals in the various stages of processing, unless they are certified organic. Even natural, un-dyed fabrics like linen may have been treated with substances which can cause allergic reactions in some people and, if not carefully managed, could have caused pollution in the growing or production cycle.

Formaldehyde

This potentially toxic chemical is used in certain fabric finishing processes, mainly to reduce wrinkling or static cling, and to provide stain and chlorine resistance. Although its use is now restricted, it is probably still used in some parts of the world. It also takes several washes to remove formaldehyde from fabrics, unlike other treatments which are more easily washed out. Organic fabrics are not treated with formaldehyde.

Chlorine bleach

Few fibres are naturally white. To commercially achieve plain white fabric it is often chlorine-bleached. Not only does this create potential environmental damage during production, it also continues to release gas when we wear or use the bleached fabric, and some people are concerned that this is harmful. Look for non-chlorine-bleached fabrics or natural un-dyed fabrics. Organic fabrics should not be chlorine bleached.

Dyes

Commercial fabrics are dyed using synthetic chemicals, mainly derived from petrochemicals. In the past, naturally-occurring substances – either plant- or animal-based – were used to colour cloth. In the 19th century, artificial colours were created using processed petrochemicals and these days almost all fabrics are dyed with synthetic chemicals. Many dyes are made with potentially polluting metals such as zinc, copper and chromium. While developed countries now have stringent protections in place, developing countries may not have the same safeguards either for worker health or water pollution. Steps can be taken by fabric dyers to minimise the impact of the dye bath, by ensuring that little or no waste is produced and that the remaining residue is safely treated. Old, often-washed fabrics will have less dye (and other) chemical residues in them – another argument for the use of recycled fabrics.

Home treatments for fabrics

It is possible to buy all sorts of sprays and treatments for fabrics, from starch for stiffening cloth to anti-static spray to stop fabrics clinging.

Starch is a naturally-occurring chemical from plants, and is used to stiffen fabrics. It was traditionally used for tablelinen and napkins as well as other linens. Natural starch is pretty harmless and can be used to make floaty or slippery fabrics easier to handle. Several different types of fabric spray are available, like fabric stiffener made from PVA (poly-vinyl acrylic) glue, designed to permanently stiffen fabrics for roller blinds and craft use. Other types of stiffeners or stabilisers are designed to temporarily stiffen fabric to make it easy to handle, then they wash out after use. One product (Palmer Pletch Perfect Sew) claims to be non-toxic, non-allergenic and environmentally-safe.

Fire retardants

In industrial use, many soft furnishings will be treated with fire retardants and there is some concern about the health impacts of these. The EU is legislating to ban the types of fire retardants that are now known to be toxic.

Stain protection treatments

There is ongoing debate (including in the European Parliament) about the possible risks to health of using treatments that may contain formaldehyde or perfluorcarbons, which have been linked to health risks.

Is organic better?

Ethical consumers are becoming increasingly aware of the benefits of organic products, particularly in regard to food. We want to reduce the number and amount of chemicals we ingest through our food and particularly in what we feed to our children. We also want to reduce the impact on the land from the use of agricultural chemicals. Slowly but steadily, the same awareness is creeping into our clothing choices. Many people would prefer to use organic cotton for baby clothes, aware of the residual chemicals in standard fabrics which may cause allergic reactions or other health issues. The same applies to all our clothes, household furnishings and bedding. We want the best and the safest for our families, and of course we enjoy the added benefit of knowing that our organic choices also have a positive impact on the environment in terms of chemical use.

However, bear in mind the downsides of organic fabrics:

✳ Many will have been grown and produced thousands of miles away and have been transported long distances.

✳ 'Organic' is not the same as 'fairtrade', although there is often a lot of crossover. The product is not guaranteed fairtrade unless it has the accreditation.

✳ Organic fabrics are usually more expensive than their non-organic counterparts. This is an important factor when choosing what to buy to make something. Think of it in the same way as buying good organic food; yes it costs more, but you can have a beautiful home-cooked organic meal instead of eating out. Buy less but buy better.

ALTERNATIVE ECO BRANDING

Locally-produced
Some products will be marketed as 'eco' simply because they are produced locally. While local production is excellent news in terms of air-miles, other factors such as chemical use should also be taken into account.

Un-dyed/Limited processing/Natural fibres
Some products may be sold as natural, therefore eco. Again, just because something hasn't been dyed doesn't mean it hasn't been subject to chemical processing, energy-consuming transport or unjust working practices.

Organic fabrics

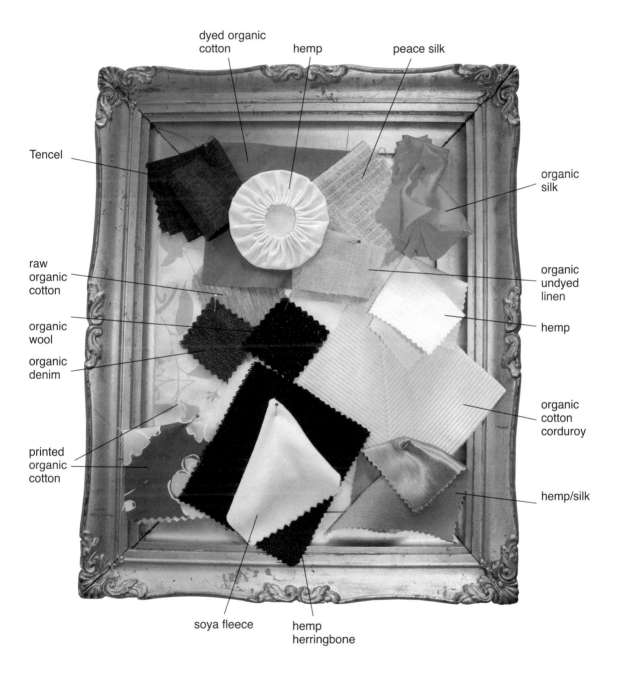

dyed organic cotton

hemp

peace silk

Tencel

organic silk

raw organic cotton

organic undyed linen

organic wool

hemp

organic denim

organic cotton corduroy

printed organic cotton

hemp/silk

soya fleece

hemp herringbone

Energy and water resources

The two precious resources we need to consider in textile production are water and energy (mainly fossil fuel-derived). Confusingly, some synthetic fibres may appear lower-impact than natural fibres when their whole production is considered, particularly in terms of energy and resource use. It takes thousands of litres of water to produce one kilo of cotton but almost none to produce the same amount of polyester fibre. However, polyester uses petrochemicals as its source, and twice as much energy is required to produce a kilo of polyester than to produce a kilo of cotton. So which is more eco? To make things even more confusing, polyester and other synthetic fibres are easy-care and so use fewer resources in their final-product use. We wash them on low temperatures, they dry quickly and they need little ironing, so in many ways they are lower-impact than natural fibres. But they are created either from petrochemicals or using processes requiring extensive chemical solvents (in the case of cellulose-based fabrics like viscose or bamboo).

Other energy uses in textile production include:

* manufacture of agricultural chemicals;
* water for irrigation and associated transport costs;
* petrochemicals for agricultural machinery and onward transport;
* energy use and water in processing; and
* transport of product to various stages of processing.

Organic and low-impact production methods cut out a significant portion of the energy consumed, but still cannot usually be considered carbon-neutral.

Transport of fabrics is a major issue; fabrics and clothes are rarely made in the same country as that in which the fibre is produced. Fibres, fabrics and finished goods may well travel thousands of miles around the world even before they begin their journey from shop to wardrobe. Locally-made fabrics start to look increasingly attractive when we consider the fabric-miles travelled by other fabrics.

Synthetic fabrics

Most synthetic fabrics (polyester, nylon, acrylic and derivatives) are made from petrochemicals. There is no doubt that the use of such petrochemicals is an environmental issue. However, in terms of fabric production, synthetics generally use much less energy to make and to care for. Their production cycle isn't so intensive as that of cotton, it produces fewer emissions and pollutants than the cycles of most natural fibres and the finished garments are easier to care for, requiring less water and energy use in the home. On the downside, synthetic fabrics are not biodegradable so they last pretty much forever in landfill.

But can synthetics be considered eco? Fabrics consuming less energy in their production processes are definitely an important eco-sewing choice. As we have seen, organic fabrics use fewer resources. Locally-produced fabrics require less transport energy. Synthetics generally require less processing energy but they are made from petrochemicals – a non-sustainable source. The choice you should make is not always clear, as there is not just one easy answer; it is instead a matter of discovering the facts and making your own choices according to your priorities.

Recycled fabrics

Fabrics made from recycled materials are extremely rare and are hard to buy retail. The most commonly discussed recycled fibre is polyester which is indefinitely recyclable and can be made from polyester fabric as well as from plastic bottles. The energy used to collect and re-use polyester is massively less than that required for new polyester to be created. Therefore polyester fabric should be highly sustainable, but the process is not fully developed and certainly not commercial. It is possible to recycle natural fabrics by pulling them apart and re-spinning the fibre, but this creates low-quality fabric for which there is limited commercial use. It has not been possible to find a source of recycled polyester fabric in the UK although there are sources in the US.

Fairtrade and ethical production

For several years now there has been intense media coverage of human rights abuses in clothing manufacture in the developing world. General textile production itself hasn't come under the same kind of scrutiny as have some of the high-profile brand names, but many of the same concerns surely apply. It is very difficult to discover the production source of fabrics in most shops. Fabrics are sold to wholesalers who then sell on to the shops, with the result that the consumers are very removed from the actual production process. Fabrics made in the UK, USA and Europe should have been produced in good working conditions. However, we cannot be so sure that textiles sold incredibly cheaply by retailers have been produced in conditions we could deem acceptable.

The Fairtrade brand allows us to choose fabrics and other products which have been assessed as being produced with fair prices, with sustainability in mind and in decent working conditions. Fairtrade accreditation is still very rare for fabrics and non-accredited fabrics may well have been produced in conditions as good as or even exceeding fairtrade standards, although they do not have the

Recycled fabrics

sari fabric

wedding dress fabrics

corduroy shirt

dress cotton

recycled wool felt

silk scarf

bedlinen

leather sample

curtains

polar fleece

blanket

sari fabric

t-shirt jersey

devoré scarf

official mark. By choosing fairtrade we are supporting producers in the developing world but our options are very limited if we choose to use only certified fabrics. At present in the UK, Bishopstone Clothing is the main retailer of Indian fairtrade organic cotton, although other retailers also sell this and other fairtrade fabrics. Until there is a greater transparency and more choice available for consumers, you should ask for as much information as you can obtain from your fabric supplier about where fabrics were made, then use your own judgement or stick with known, accredited sources.

Organic and recycled fabrics

Reducing waste and consumption: buy less, buy better

The textile and fashion industry is one of the most wasteful industries in the world. In the UK, one million tonnes of textiles are thrown away each year, making up 10% of domestic waste. Only 25% is reclaimed and recycled, although the vast majority could be re-purposed in some way.

Over the last 20 years, the real cost of clothing has dropped dramatically, paving the way for mass-produced disposable clothing from discount retailers including supermarkets. We, as a society, have become used to cheap clothes and are now accustomed to constantly replacing them as we grow out of them, when they need a repair, or even just because we have grown

New, vintage and recycled fabrics

Vintage embroidered linen tablecloth

bored of them. Clothes are so cheap it is easier to send an unwanted or damaged item to a charity shop and buy something new than to learn the skills and find the time to revive it. Worse still, millions of useable items of clothing are sent to landfill every year.

Stepping out of this cycle of a cheap and abundant supply of clothing is difficult, but by sewing our own we are making a positive step in the right direction – as long as we don't just create even more clothes we hardly ever wear and then send to the charity shop!

Weighing up costs against environmental concerns

Buy some lovely, expensive organic or vintage fabric and make a really special dress or a set of beautiful organic cotton bedlinens that will last for years, rather than buying three lots of cheap polyester for several dresses which you only wear a few times, or cheap supermarket poly-cotton bedlinen that will need replacing in a year or two. We all know it makes sense to buy better quality goods which will last for a long time. We just have to get used to the idea that we can't be constantly acquiring new things just because we have grown bored. Learn how to refurbish, revive and rejuvenate old things and keep them forever. And keep off the organic cake so that special dress fits you for years to come as well!

All in all, the standard textile industry doesn't emerge too well from our ethical and environmental inspection. Yet the industry supports millions of workers all over the world who depend on the trade to feed and house their families. How can we claim to be ethical and environmental if we refuse to consume their products? There are no easy answers to this – it is all too inextricably linked to the global economy for one solo eco sewer to make a significant impact. But by making conscious and careful choices in our own lives, we make a bigger impact together on the world market. As the demand for organic and low-impact production expands, so eventually the investment in producing for this market must increase.

Vintage fabrics

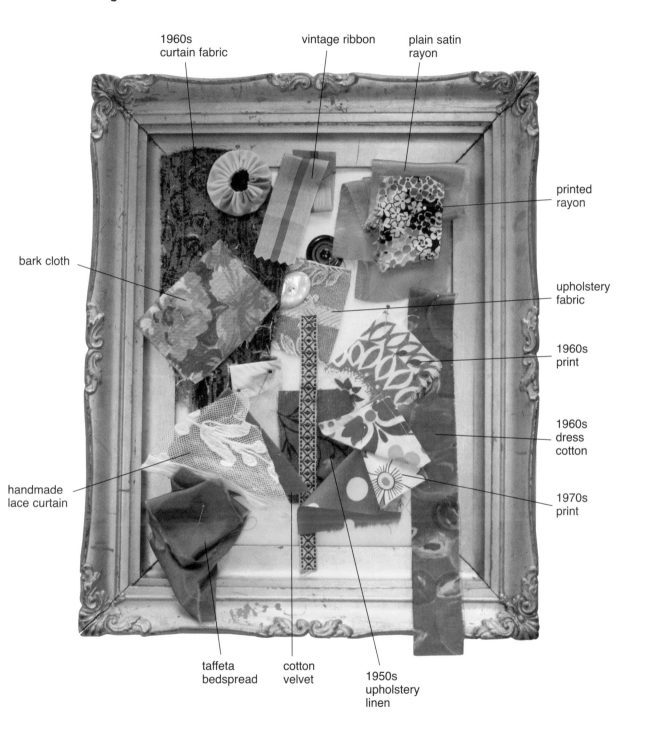

1960s curtain fabric

vintage ribbon

plain satin rayon

printed rayon

bark cloth

upholstery fabric

1960s print

1960s dress cotton

handmade lace curtain

1970s print

taffeta bedspread

cotton velvet

1950s upholstery linen

2 Buying fabrics

When we choose fabrics in the shop, it is difficult to discover the back-story behind the fabric: who made it, where was it made, what was it made with and how did it get here? Until all products are sold with their carbon footprint or production history attached, it can be very hard to decide to take one over the other in terms of eco choices. It is almost impossible to find one fabric that doesn't have some kind of impact on the environment so we have to be realistic and make choices about which of the issues matters most to each of us individually. Knowing where to start can be a little overwhelming. Should you only use organic fabrics from the other side of the world or should you use locally-made non-organic fabrics that haven't travelled so many air-miles? You might have heard about the new sustainable wonder fabric, bamboo, and be wondering if that is the answer. Or should you just stick with vintage and second-hand fabrics? Which really is the greener choice? I'm afraid there is no easy answer. Deciding what is and isn't green is a matter of personal choice and depends on your own priorities. But you can't start to make those choices without understanding the facts, so what follows is an explanation of eco sewing as I see it. These are my thoughts and opinions and you need to make up your own mind. It is not that difficult to start making some small changes to what you buy, which will have an impact on the carbon footprint of your sewing. Explore the options within this book and make the changes that work for you, your budget and your lifestyle. You can find more detail on different types of fabric and environmental impacts of each starting on p.11.

What is an eco textile?

All sorts of products and raw materials are now labelled and marketed as eco or green. Sometimes it can be hard to unpick exactly what factors support the advertised label of 'green' and even harder to assess whether it really does mean 'green'. Organic certification is great in that it guarantees the fabric has been produced in a chemical-free way, without pesticides, fertilisers and processing

ETHICAL AND ENVIRONMENTAL ISSUES

The textile and fashion industries are fraught with potential environmental and ethical issues. Some you may want to consider in your sewing, and indeed the rest of your life, are:

- chemical use in fabric production;
- fair and ethical working practices for producers;
- the burden of waste textiles in landfill;
- the use of precious non-renewable resources;
- pollution caused by production of textiles;
- the amount of energy used to produce, process and transport fabrics; and
- the amount of water used in textile production and processing.

chemicals, which was covered in Chapter 1. Other fabrics may be low-impact in different ways – they may be produced sustainably with low chemical and water use, like hemp (see p.12) or made from locally-produced materials, meaning they have fewer air-miles. Many people think natural fibres like cotton, wool, linen and silk are inherently more environmentally-friendly than synthetics because they are natural and sustainable. Natural fibres are generally better for our bodies as they allow the skin to breathe and so they seem much more eco. However, natural fibres, even if they are undyed, don't necessarily have a low impact on the environment and indeed many concerns have been raised about the health implications for both the workers farming and processing the fabrics and for those who wear the finished goods.

Chemical-free

The organic certification process costs money and small producers can't always afford it, so what we might be happy with as 'all-but-organic' isn't always officially certified as such. Small producers may state that their fabric is chemical-free or eco while not being officially organic. It is up to you, the consumer, to find out as much as you want and satisfy yourself that their claims are supported by evidence – on the whole, such producers are serious and dedicated to the welfare of their flock and crops and to reducing chemical use in their materials. Supporting small producers who are making positive changes to textile production is a really important part of being eco. See p.29 for more information.

Energy and waste

You may also want to think about the embedded energy or carbon footprint of the fabric in the shops. How much energy was used to grow or process the raw material, how intensive was the processing, how far has it travelled? Waste is another issue worth considering. The textile and fashion industries are hugely wasteful and massive amounts of fabrics end up in landfill. You may feel that using existing, second-hand or waste fabrics is a better use of resources than working with newly-produced fabrics, organic or not.

Organic & sustainable

If chemicals and pollution are your main concern, then buying organic fabrics will be high on your list of priorities. Few mainstream fabric shops sell organic fabrics, but it is always worth asking as otherwise there is no evidence of consumer demand. Most ecofibre retailers sell online or by mail order. See the suppliers list on pp. 139. Many of the organic fabric retailers also sell sustainable fabrics such as bamboo.

Locally produced

Most of the fabrics we can buy are produced in other parts of the world and are transported for sale. As with food, the less distance the fabric travels the smaller its carbon footprint. So one of the things you might like to explore to make your sewing more green is locally-produced fabrics. Britain has a long tradition of weaving and knitting wool fabric, particularly in Yorkshire and Scotland. Some manufacturers will sell direct to the public, so it's worth exploring and saving on the carbon footprint of the fabric being driven around the country. Linen is also still produced in Ireland and there are lots of fabrics produced in the EU and US, so there is no need to buy from the other side of the world if you don't want to. Eastern European countries, particularly Romania and Poland, produce a lot of hemp fabrics. Fabric shops don't always know where their fabrics were made, but try asking and see what you can find out. Remember that the fabric may well be manufactured in one place using materials from another, such as Italian cotton – the raw materials will have been imported before the cloth is woven in Italy. There are of course counter-arguments against only buying locally-made products; if we stop buying from producers in developing countries, millions of textile workers lose their employment and international trade will suffer.

Local independent shops

Supporting your local small shops, even if they don't sell organic or fair trade fabrics, is an important part of eco sewing. Keeping small shops alive is vital in encouraging more people to sew and in raising their awareness about consumption. These shops are customer-focused and potentially responsive to your needs, as well as being a fabulous source of advice and help. Talk to them about organic fabrics, ask if they can stock them. Ask whether their buyers can look for local fabrics that haven't travelled the world, or fabrics which have fair-trade certification or are industry waste materials (see below).

Small producers

Skip the corporate giants and buy direct from small-scale makers. Hunt around locally and you may well find small producers making wonderful screenprinted or hand-woven fabrics on a small scale. While these might seem relatively expensive, bear in mind the unique nature of the fabrics and the environmental benefits of supporting small producers and buying local. Many small producers take ethical and environmental issues seriously. You could also explore small producers selling online on sites like Etsy.com. (See Suppliers section pp. 139.) New organic fabrics are becoming available all the time.

Digital print

There are some strong arguments in favour of digital printing as an eco method for decorating cloth. Because the printers only print the exact amount you require, there is no waste. Digital print also avoids the risk of ink pollutants entering watercourses and of waste ink needing disposal after the printing process. Other techniques are being developed which give a low-impact printing technique. Digital print services are becoming increasingly available. You can choose or create your own design and have it printed on the cloth of your choice. Ask about having it printed on organic cotton or see whether you can supply your own fabric.

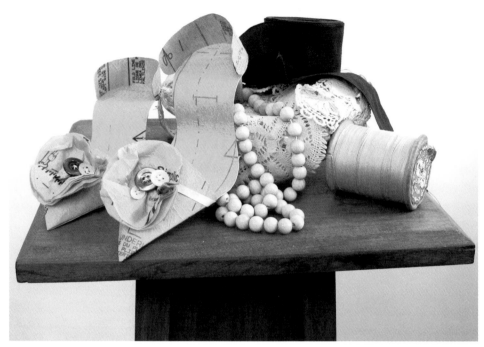

Paper shoes by Jennifer Collier

Pre-consumer waste

Both the clothing and the furnishings industries create a lot of waste fabric. This is known in the recycling trade as 'pre-consumer waste', as it hasn't gone through the retail trade.

Industry waste

Huge over-runs in production can leave bolts of top-quality fabrics unused and unwanted by the manufacturer. Despite the fact that it costs money to send this to landfill many companies still do, particularly with smaller pieces, as it takes time and effort to find a productive use for it. Many independent fabric shops and market traders buy their fabric stocks from industry over-runs. These can be stunning designer fabrics and available in large quantities. Talk to your local supplier to find out what they have and what else they might be able to source. Craft supplies shows often have fabric stalls selling designer over-runs.

Scrap stores

Some manufacturers donate their unused fabrics and other materials to local scrap stores, which are usually set up for schools and community groups to use for craft materials. Some allow access to individual artists and families for a small charge and they can be an excellent source of fabrics, haberdashery and weird and wonderful industrial bits and bobs.

Seconds
Another source of waste fabrics is slight seconds – a designer or good quality fabric, with a slight print or weave flaw. Independent fabric shops often sell designer seconds fabrics at excellent prices. While this might be a problem for curtains or tablecloths, when you are making clothes or small projects it is easy enough to work around a stain or flaw. Just make sure you check first and buy extra fabric if necessary.

Independent designers
If you are after small pieces of fabric, talk to local designers about their scraps. It is likely that they produce a sizable quantity of scraps they don't know what to do with, and these can be fabulous fabrics. Some may even have large pieces they will happily sell or swap for something else.

Post-consumer waste
Post-consumer waste is any fabric that has already been bought and sold before – in effect secondhand, rather than left-overs from manufacture.

Secondhand
Given the amount of energy and resources going into fabric production, even organic, where possible I always prefer to use secondhand fabrics. Shopping secondhand is never predictable; you have to make do with what you can find, rather than hunting for the exact colour and pattern you have in mind. Secondhand shopping can open your imagination to new patterns, fabrics and colours you might not otherwise have considered.

Buying second-hand fabrics
For dressmaking and large projects you have two options: either pre-cut vintage dressmaking fabrics or large pieces of second-hand fabric from various sources. While it used to be possible to buy fabrics easily in charity shops, it's getting increasingly rare to find them, as shops don't stock what they think won't sell. Get to know the shop managers and ask them to keep fabrics aside for you. Independent shops are often better than the big charity names. Small towns are often the best places to find independent charity shops and local knowledge is

very useful in discovering the places most likely to yield good fabric supplies. Many vintage clothes shops will keep a stock of fabrics, at least in storage if not in their shop. Keep in touch with them and find out when new things become available. Other junk shops, antique shops and flea market stalls may well have access to vintage fabrics so check them all regularly and keep an eye out. If you have the time and commitment, you can hunt down amazing fabrics at good prices by going to auctions and talking direct to house clearance companies, but unless you want masses, it is easier to go through a dealer of some sort, who will have done all the leg work,

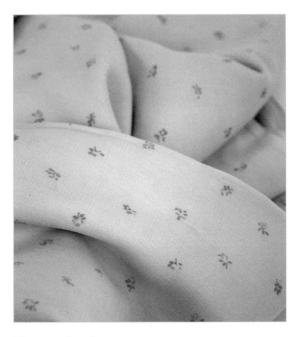

Vintage printed rayon

made all the contacts and presented the fabric nicely for sale. Car boot sales can sometimes be a great source of vintage fabrics if you strike it lucky and find someone clearing out granny's sewing room. Go to your local sales often and talk to the regulars to find out whether any are house clearance or second-hand dealers.

Ebay is an excellent source of vintage and second-hand fabrics, though you are buying fabric unseen and of course untouched. It may look nice in the picture and feel horrible! Be aware that many sellers, even those who are dealers, may not always know what it is they have got and can mis-describe the fibre content. You may end up with rayon which the dealer, in all honesty, thought was silk. It is sometimes hard to know what an unlabelled, fifty-year-old piece of fabric actually is.

Upcycling

Upcycling means using something that was a waste material to make something of a higher value. So by thinking laterally

Recycled blanket

Sari

Vintage bedspread

about what we use as fabric, we can upcycle all sorts of things. You don't
necessarily need a piece of dressmaking fabric to make your planned project,
even if it needs quite large pieces. Other sources of fabric might include:

* bedlinen
* curtains
* curtain linings
* saris & sarongs
* throws and blankets
* large garments.

If you are struggling to find large pieces of fabric in the colours and patterns
you want, think about dyeing, printing and hand-painting recycled fabrics to
create what you are looking for. Embroidery and other embellishments can
transform a plain piece of sheeting into a one-off treasure.

Bedlinen
Bedlinen can be really useful. Don't be too squeamish about bedsheets, but do
inspect before you buy – there is no point in having something stained and off-
putting! Double duvet covers are huge pieces of fabric and can be really useful.

Turn them inside out, with the corners turned right out (to make sure there is no fluff stuck in the seams!) and wash them on a low heat with washing balls (see p.45), then line dry to give them a good airing. I use bedlinen to make toiles (test-versions of clothes) to check the fit, rather than use new fabric. Some small-scale patterns on bedlinen can be very effective, but be wary of big bold prints which will just make you look like you are wearing a duvet cover! Plain pastel coloured sheets and duvet covers are the most commonly available but quality will vary enormously. Look for the heavier-weight fabrics or ones that feel nicest, rather than cheap, thin polycotton, which will always look and feel like cheap, thin polycotton. It is increasingly hard to find real, sturdy cotton sheets, but it is still worth looking. Antique and junk shops are sometimes better places for finding these than charity shops. Even pillowcases can be useful. Pretty patterned ones turn up quite often and have a good amount of fabric in them – enough to make a top or even a simple short skirt. Bright or strong coloured bedding is hard to come by, so snap it up when you see it. Most charity shops don't sell wool blankets on open sale because of fire-safety regulations. Ask staff about wool blankets for dog bedding and you may have more luck.

Curtains

Curtains are a traditional source of dressmaking fabric – made famous by Scarlett O'Hara and Maria Von Trapp! The only real problem with using curtain fabric (apart from the constant comments about looking like a sofa) is the possibility that the fabric is damaged. Curtains which have hung in the sunlight for years will have been damaged and the fabric weakened, even if this doesn't show initially. Generally the first thing you should do with old curtains is wash them. If the curtains are old, and weren't lined, they could well disintegrate. Hand washing will preserve delicate fabrics better than even the gentlest washing machine cycle. The fabric of lined curtains will usually only degrade on the exposed edges, which will often be faded as well. So you may be lucky and find that the centre part of the curtain fabric is in good condition. The top and bottom hem are usually not much use either – the hem is likely to be dirty or faded, and the fold line will show when you unfold the hem. The gathered part at the top is also likely to be creased and faded. This area gathers the most dust, so it may be stained as well. Before washing, undo all the hems and remove the linings and rufflette tape. You can usually unpick the start of the stitching and then simply rip the tape off. If the fabric tears, you will know you have a weak material and handwashing might be the only way to keep it intact. If it seems sturdy or the curtains fairly new or little used, then the fabric is probably strong enough for you to just rip the seams open and fling it all in the washing machine. Of course, if the curtains are very dusty you should wash them before you do any ripping up, or that dust will go everywhere including into your lungs. You might prefer to work outside. Always undo the rufflette tape so the gathers open up. You can keep the rufflette tape to re-use for other curtains and crafts projects.

Vintage and antique fabrics

Vintage embroideries

Some of the most common textile items you will find secondhand are hand-embroidered tablecloths, tray cloths, napkins and lace or crochet doilies. Some people like to collect them and keep them as sourcebooks of embroidery patterns and stitches, but if you want to cut them up and use them then do so. Embroideries were usually stitched with colour-fast threads so they can be safely washed.

Antique fabrics

Sometimes, if you are lucky, you will come upon a real fabric treasure – something rare and very special. 'Vintage' is so fashionable and saleable a label that anything pre-1985 is called vintage. That may well include rare and valuable pre-1930s fabrics, or even 18th- and 19th-century fabrics. As most people can't tell the difference, all sorts of fabrics get bundled into the 'vintage' bracket, whether or not they are special or even old. Retro-style prints, replicating much older fabrics, can get mixed up with real vintage. If you think you have found something really special or unusual, try to have it checked out by a specialist before you do anything with it. Many museum services have a textiles curator so you could take the fabric along to one of their identification days and ask them to take a look, or you could try sending a good photo and description to the nearest specialist. Always try your local museum service before you go to a major institution. Auction houses can provide identification and valuation, while museums don't give valuations. So if you have established that you have something very special, it is up to you to decide what to do with it. If you want to keep it as a specimen then do, but if you really want to make a dress out of it, then why not? But do check whether it is valuable before you slice into it and be aware that old fabrics are fragile and may not withstand construction and wearing. If what you have is small scraps or a damaged piece of cloth then you might as well incorporate it into something new and special – even just a pincushion. Enjoy it!

Embroidered tablecloth

Lace

What fabric-oholic doesn't have a box of vintage lace knocking around somewhere? Many of us just hoard pieces of lace and pull the boxes out to show other obsessives. But unless you are a serious collector with a specialist interest, really the lace is there to be used. As with fabrics, check with a specialist if you think you have something really special, but otherwise just enjoy it. The Lace Bag project on p.108 was designed specially to make use of delicate vintage lace motifs. (Also see Buying Vintage Fabrics, p.48.)

Recycling clothing

Large-size garments are a great source of fabrics for crafts and small projects. Men's shirts yield good size panels from the back and smaller pieces from the front and sleeves. Skirts are also great, particularly long, simple-cut ones made from large pieces of fabric rather than a number of panels sewn together, and the same applies to dresses. Jackets and trousers are not so good for

Antique lace

large pieces of fabrics, as they are made up from small sections, but if you use small pieces then jackets can be a fantastic source for wool suiting, tweeds and heavier fabrics like denim, corduroy and velvet. Wool coats can be very useful; again look for those made of large areas of un-seamed fabric. Like wool jumpers, wool coating can be felted (see next page). Wedding-dresses, bridesmaids' dresses and evening dresses often have masses of useable fabric in their skirts, and once they are out of style, they can be be bought cheaply in charity shops. Beware of the fibre content though – material labelled as satin might be polyester or silk. But if you like the look and the feel of the fabric then that's what matters.

Vintage printed wool

To extract the best from garments, wash and line dry before you start cutting up. Then cut along all the main seams and remove waistbands, cuffs, collars and buttons. Keep any useable parts like buttons and zips. Unpicking a zip is tiresome, but if the garment used an invisible zip (as good quality skirts often do), you can save money the next time you need one. Linings can also be useful fabrics. It is often worth extracting a skirt lining in one piece by unpicking the waist seams so it can be used again, rather than cutting it up. Suede and leather garments are best unpicked rather than cut, so you have the most useable fabric from them.

Recycled wedding dress fabric

Making wool felt from recycled jumpers

Wool jumpers can be felted in a domestic washing machine to create lovely colourful wool felt for all sorts of projects from appliqué (see p.64) to tea cosies (p.76). Wool felt doesn't fray and, because it has already been washed is also washable, so can be used for appliqué on clothes.

The first stage is to find suitable jumpers, which isn't always that easy. The best jumpers are at least 75% wool or other animal fibre such as cashmere or angora. A small percentage of synthetic shouldn't make a difference. What really matters is that the jumper should be handwash only. Some wool is pre-treated so it can be easily machine washed without shrinking. Felting is just planned shrinking, so untreated, handwash-only jumpers will yield the best results. Felting is always unpredictable so the only thing to do is experiment. Plain knit jumpers work best and produce a smooth fabric. Aran knit and cable patterns will still be visible after felting and the thicker the original knit, the thicker the felt will be. Experiment with a few to find out what sort of felt you prefer.

Hand-knit jumpers often felt wonderfully but as they have no labels, you cannot accurately predict whether they will felt or not. Ribbing on the hems and cuffs usually doesn't felt very well. Whole jumpers can be washed individually but this isn't very efficient use of the energy and water in the wash cycle. So, if you can, save up several and put them all in together; but make sure you use some kind of dye-catcher cloth or the colours will run and create a lot of sludge-coloured wool felt. Your usual biodegradable washing detergent will work fine, although you could experiment with home-made natural detergents (see p.46).

If you wish, you can put the jumpers in with other laundry, but to prevent loose wool fluff attaching itself to everything else in the wash, you should first put the jumpers in an old pillowcase and tie this tightly with string. Again, use a dye catcher or the jumpers will bleed dye into your other laundry. There is no need to wash them on the highest temperature. Most wool jumpers will felt on 60°C, though some will work on 40°C. If they fail to felt the first time, put them back through another wash. You might like to include washing balls (see p.45) or old tennis balls to increase the chances of felting. Don't use fabric conditioner if you think you might need to felt them a second time – sometimes it inhibits felting. Try using a couple of tablespoons of white vinegar in the conditioner slot. I've never tumble-dried wool felt, although other people swear by it. I personally think there is no need and you might as well be even more eco and not use a drier. Always take the wool felt out of the machine as soon as the wash has finished, to prevent creases setting in. If you find that sleeves dry with a ridge down the fold, try cutting them off and opening them out flat before you wash the jumper. Many books about felting are for American readers and talk about top-loading washing machines where you can stop the wash and check the progress of your felting part-way through. With British (front-loading) machines, there is no way to do this so you just have to hope it works!

Once the jumper is felted and shrunk (usually down to child-size from adult-size) dry it and then cut into sections along the seams. A warm steam iron is the best way to eradicate creases so you end up with flat pieces of felt. Beware of using an iron that is too hot with any jumper containing a percentage of synthetic fibre as these will melt onto your iron. Sometimes you may want to leave the ribbing on the hem and cuffs and incorporate them into your project, but if not, cut them off and save for other things. It is worth keeping all the scraps, particularly those of attractive colours, to use for appliqué or brooches. When cutting out detailed shapes, try the freezer paper technique explained on p.66. It is difficult to make marks on felt using tailors' chalk, so I use soap – the last thin slivers of a dry, well-used bar works perfectly on fluffy fabrics.

Recycled wool felt

NB. If you do a lot of felting, be sure to check your washing machine's filter regularly and clear out the lint as often as necessary.

3 Making greener choices in your sewing practice

We have looked at making your fabric-acquiring more green and environmentally aware, so what about the rest of your sewing necessities; what choices can you make with haberdashery and other materials?

Interfacing

Interfacing is a layer of fabric used inside clothing and in some crafts to strengthen and support fabrics so they keep their shape. It is most common on cuffs and collars in tailored clothes. Interfacing is also used to stiffen fabric for handbags, to make it more durable, and for appliqué, to make cut-out shapes less likely to fray and easier to sew down.

There are two main types of interfacing: traditional fabrics like cotton or horsehair, and synthetic materials which can have a heat-activated glue backing. Non-woven interfacing, the type which is most commonly available with a glue backing, is made from polyester from petrochemicals. Although the technology exists to recycle polyester (such as plastic drinks bottles) to make polyester fibre, fabrics and interfacing made from recycled polyester are not yet widely commercially available. Iron-on interfacing can be tricky to use; it is good for crafts but potentially more problematic in dressmaking. It can shrink, causing the fabric to wrinkle, or it can bubble, fail to stick properly, change the feel of the fabric, show through from the front side, shred or even detach in use. Given the unknown glue which is used to create the heat-activated bond, you may prefer to use alternatives to make your sewing greener.

Woven interfacing materials vary; some is made from natural fibres, usually cotton, while some is synthetic. Either can be made with the iron-on glue. Hair canvas has been used for hundreds of years to stiffen tailored clothes and can be used in crafts as well. It can be made from goat and horse hair, sometimes combined with wool or rayon. It is stiff, scratchy and quite expensive, but if you want to eliminate synthetics then this is a good choice. Some 'horse hair' canvas is wholly or partly made from plastics, too. Information about the source of the animal fibre is rather hard to discover. Vegans may prefer to use a vegetable fibre. As an alternative to ready-made interfacing, you can use other traditional fabrics like horsehair as sew-in interfacing. Fine organic cotton or voile would work for lightweight projects like dressmaking, and heavy hemp canvas could be used as stronger support for crafts or tailoring. You could also re-use old sheets or even garments where smaller pieces are needed. Other options include organic cotton flannel or recycled (or even organic) wool for a thicker interfacing. Recycled fleece fabric is lightweight; small pieces can be obtained from old clothes and larger pieces from old blankets, rather than buying new. Fleece-type fabric made from cotton or hemp is also available. Try using traditional hessian for heavy-duty crafts and pelmets rather than plastic interfacing.

Wadding and interlining

If you make quilts, you will know that the most widely available and affordable form of wadding for the inside of quilts is polyester wadding or batting. Alternatives are available, including cotton and organic cotton as well as pure wool – these have the added advantage of being natural, breathable fibres. Silk wadding is also sometimes available and new eco waddings made from bamboo and recycled polyester are now available. Cotton wadding isn't too much more expensive than polyester, although silk and wool can be very pricy. Other options you may like to explore, depending on the type of projects you are making, are re-used fleece blanket, wool blankets or sustainable fabrics such as organic cotton flannel or cotton/hemp fleece. Experiment with the alternatives to find one which has the right weight and drape for your project.

Vintage thread stand

Stuffing for cushions and crafts

Ready-made cushion inners are polyester, which, as we have seen, isn't the most sustainable fibre. There are a few options you might like to consider for making more eco-friendly cushion inners:

1. Re-use. Old cushion inners might be flat, grubby and unappealing, but washing will freshen them up. Put the whole cushion inner in the washing machine, or wash by hand and then air dry. Cut open and remove the filling and pull apart to fluff up, tearing the filling into small pieces; the air between the fibres is what makes the filling lofty and fluffy and the fibres do become compressed with use. You can also do the same with polyester-filled pillows and even duvets if you want a lot of stuffing. Make a new cover to the dimensions required from organic or clean, re-used cloth such as old bedlinen, leaving a gap on one side. Stuff the filling back in carefully, using small pieces to avoid lumps and sew up the opening.

2. Make cushion covers as above and fill with organic or sustainable filling. There are many different sorts of filling available at a range of prices, though none could be called cheap. Organic wool balls are ideal for filling cushions, as are latex chips, though they make very heavy cushions. Modern fibres such as Ingeo made from maize (see p.14) are available in the US and may soon be sold in the UK, along with organic cotton and wool stuffing and hemp fibre.

3. When making small toys or pincushions you can try all sorts of different stuffing. Recycled cushion filling (see above) is a good choice as it is easily washable, but you can also use sewing scraps for things you don't intend to wash (see p.44).

More eco sewing tips

Plastic boning
When making bags or other items that require plastic boning, consider using strips of the stiff, flat plastic tape which is used on the outside of parcels. It works very well for stiffening handbag handles. Ask people who receive office deliveries and they should be able to find some for you.

Vintage toy sewing machine

Vintage scissors and thimbles

Piping cord

Until organic piping cord is produced, consider using another type of sustainable yarn such as organic cotton knitting yarn. If the yarn isn't thick enough to replace the weight of piping cord you require, twist lengths together to make thicker cord.

Embroidery threads

Collect a stock of old threads from charity shops to use for embroidery. Work with what you have rather than buying a whole skein of new thread for every project – sometimes you only need a small amount of a colour for a planned project, which can leave you with a lot of wasted threads. Also consider using fine wool threads, particularly organic knitting yarn. Go to craft shows and markets to find small producers using natural dyes or locally-produced yarns.

Recycle

Use old shirts to make cushion covers (see p.96). Use old bedlinen to make test-fit clothes or toiles.

Waste

Textiles account for a huge amount of landfill waste in the UK. By re-using old fabrics and up-cycling second-hand clothes, we can reduce the amount of useable textiles being thrown away. However, we still produce our own fabric waste and it is hard to know what is best to do with it. The following are just a few ideas; if you have others please send them in to www.seweco.co.uk:

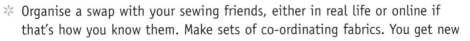

Vintage threads

❋ Organise a swap with your sewing friends, either in real life or online if that's how you know them. Make sets of co-ordinating fabrics. You get new fabric, they get new fabric and no money is spent and no fabric is wasted. Although of course it may sit in their stash for years too!

✳ Take up quilting, the traditional use for small scraps. Quilting doesn't have to involve tiny, hand-sewn patches. Contemporary patchwork can be whatever you want – use a sewing machine to piece together regular-sized squares or rectangles into striped panels then join them together. Or find a quilter who would happily use your scraps in their own work.

✳ Tiny scraps, thread ends and trimmed edges can all be saved up to use as stuffing for pincushions, stuffed toys, draught excluders and decorative cushions.

✳ Use small pieces of fabric as appliqué and to create decorative details like the blossoms adorning the skirt on p.133. Store your scraps in boxes or jars according to colour so you can easily select co-ordinating bits to go together.

✳ Offer fabric scraps to scrapstores (see p.30) or direct to local playgroups and community projects for craft activities.

✳ If you know the fibre content of the fabrics, you can look into composting natural fibres. Research into domestic composting of wool or cotton fabric is currently very limited but if you have the compost bins to experiment with you could give it a try yourself. Large amounts of wool will create ammonia which is not good, but small amounts might well decompose without any problems in your compost bin.

✳ Wool fabrics can be felted in the same way as jumpers (pp.38-9) and then used for appliqué and other crafts.

✳ Contact your local recycling centre or council facility and ask for their suggestions and recommendations. There may well be a recycling initiative locally.

✳ Keep the printed selvedges of printed fabrics to sew together and make a new fabric. Some designers have made fabulous scarves, pincushions and even dresses from the printed selvedges. (See seweco.co.uk for more information.)

Vintage patchwork pieces

* Offer fabric scraps on recycling networks like Freecycle.
* Make rag rugs.
* Tie strips onto string or ribbon to make bunting for garden parties and decorations.
* Use fabric scraps as cleaning cloths around your home and in the car.
* Donate plastic bobbins to scrap stores or playgroups for crafts projects, or search online for ways to use them yourself.
* Keep broken or bent needles and pins in a pot (I use an old film canister) and, when full, take it to the recycling centre and put in the metal bin.

Washing

For ready-made, shop-bought clothing, the largest proportion of the carbon-footprint of a garment is in the washing and drying of it in the home. Believe it or not, wherever in the world it comes from, however it is produced, if you wash it after each wear and dry it in a tumble dryer, you are creating a massive carbon-footprint for that garment. And of course this applies as much to home-made dresses or shop-bought organic cotton pyjamas. Steps have been taken by major retailers and laundry wash producers to encourage consumers to wash at cooler temperatures, and some have even started to advocate line-drying rather than tumble drying. The environmental impact of washing is one of the arguments for synthetic fabrics and other fabrics treated with stain-resistant finishes. Many synthetics are designed to be easy care, although most consumers don't know this and wash all their clothes far more regularly than they really need to. Anything which reduces the domestic carbon footprint is a good thing so being aware of the impact of washing and drying is an important part of being an eco sewer.

Wash on low temperatures
It does get things clean, really. Use washing balls to give extra pummelling to things you would normally wash on higher temperatures like bedlinen and towels. Washing balls are golf-ball sized and made of plastic; they add to the friction in the wash to beat out more dirt without the need for chemical laundry washes and higher temperatures. Some are designed to replace laundry wash while others simply add to the friction in addition to laundry wash. They are also useful for making felt (see pp.38).

Vintage ribbon

Make your own laundry wash

Making your own laundry wash is cheap, you know exactly what it contains, and you are reducing packing and transport required for bulky bottles and boxes. Look on the internet for a recipe or try the library for books on natural cleaning products (see seweco.co.uk).

Also:

* Give up your tumble dryer and install ceiling-mounted laundry racks or, ideally, use a washing line.

* Stop washing your clothes after every single wearing. Air them on the washing line or on hangers.

* Spot clean dirty marks and stains rather than throwing the whole garment in the machine.

* Keep your clothes cleaner in the first place by wearing an apron, or changing into old clothes especially set aside for the purpose before you do something grubby.

Dye your own

Ready-made dyes

It is extremely easy to dye your own fabrics using ready-made chemical dyes designed for home dyeing, or with industrial dyes (used by fashion and textile colleges and professional textile dyers). The dyes are still potentially toxic, hazardous and polluting, so exercise caution if you choose to dye fabrics yourself.

Machine-dyes are practical and easy to use, but any dye which is not taken up by the fabric will be released into the water system through your sewerage system. While domestic use isn't a major cause of water pollution, it is worth considering whether you really want to do this. Hand-dyeing in small batches using carefully-measured amounts of chemical dye can be more eco, if you are careful.

Dyes are generally pigments suspended in water, which attach themselves to the fabric. You will need the optimum amount of dye-to-fabric to achieve the strong colour as shown on the packet. A used dye-bath will still have dye suspended in the water and you can re-use the dye-bath to get gradually paler colours from it, until the dye bath is exhausted (run out of colour). Once the dye-bath is exhausted, the chemical content is pretty low and it is better to dispose of this rather than a colourful, chemically-loaded dye-bath. Only make up as much dye as you need and dye the fabric as required. Then use up the remaining dye to colour other fabrics in lighter tones until there is no colour remaining. You can always over-dye the pale colours to create yet more colours.

Natural dyes

Experimenting with natural dyes to colour cloth for your own sewing projects is enjoyable and exciting. There are many books about natural dyes, although most are about dyeing wool or silk yarn for knitting projects, rather than fabrics. Few cover the environmental consequences of natural dyeing in detail, but *Eco Colour* by India Flint is a notable exception. Natural dyes use fixatives and additives to enhance and preserve the colour, so always research the chemicals used to be sure you are happy to be using them and applying them to cloth you are going to wear or use in the home. Naturally-dyed fabrics are hard to buy commercially, but they are available from small-scale producers and specialists, though they are not cheap. Plant and animal dyes, although naturally-occurring, are still chemicals and some dyes are enhanced by potentially harmful additions such as tin or chromium to make them effective or to create a range of colours from the same dye.

The most common natural dye is indigo (which is chemically the same as woad, widely used to make coloured cloth in medieval England and, in legend, used by the ancient Britons to paint themselves blue). Indigofera is the active ingredient found in woad and several types of indigo plant around the world. It produces a strong, almost permanent, blue dye which has been used for traditional denim jeans fabric for many years. Today, a synthetic version of indigo is used commercially, rather than the plant-derived form which is complex and time-consuming to prepare. Many non-Western societies still use indigo to dye traditional fabrics, although again these are increasingly synthetic rather than real indigo. Other plant dyes are used to create a range of colours, and these are by no means dull or dingy if manipulated by an expert dyer. It can be difficult to achieve strong, consistent colours with natural dyes and it takes years of practice to understand the ways of dyestuffs.

There are also a few animal-based dyes which are quite rare but worth knowing about. Cochineal used to be a common food-colouring – giving a bright pinky-red – created from the coccus beetle, originally found in Mexico. It is possible to buy powdered cochineal to make your own dye. Murex is far less common; this purple dye is created from certain types of rare shellfish. However you dye, making responsible choices about disposing of your waste is the most important thing.

4 Buying vintage fabrics and haberdashery

There are many sorts of vintage fabrics around, anything from 19th-century printed cottons to 1980s curtain fabrics. I prefer to think of pre-1970s as vintage and pre-1930s as antique, but there isn't an official definition. My favourite fabrics to use are from the 1930s, 1940s and 1950s although I love to collect and hoard older fabrics. Before the 1960s, many fabrics were woven on narrow looms giving a maximum width (selvedge to selvedge) of about 36in./91.5cm. While fabrics were still produced in 36in./91.5cm width after the 1960s, they became less common. 1950s floral prints and '60s abstract ones are probably the most common dressmaking fabrics you will come across in vintage and antique shops, although sometimes you will find older ones, particularly pre-war printed rayon and occasionally silk. There are photos of vintage fabrics on p.25. Because of the fashions of the time, most vintage dressmaking fabrics are printed and you can get all sorts of wonderful floral and abstract prints in a whole array of different colours. Plain fabrics are less common, other than lining material or plain pastel-coloured rayon from the 1940s. Fabrics with patterns woven in are usually upholstery fabrics. Shot taffeta from the 1950s is rare but a real treasure. Some plain cotton fabrics also turn up but it is hard to date them unless they are 36in./91.5cm width or narrower. There are environmental concerns about the chemicals used in dry cleaning so I suggest careful hand washing except of very delicate items. Always use pure soap flakes, a biodegradable washing liquid, or home-made washing liquid (see p.46). Washing powder doesn't always dissolve in the cold water required for washing delicate fabrics. A tablespoonful of white vinegar in your final rinse will act as a fabric conditioner and may help to preserve dyes. Vintage fabrics should not be machine washed often as they will eventually deteriorate, and garments made from vintage fabrics should be hand washed.

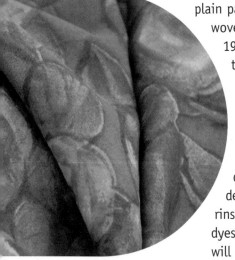

1950s printed rayon

Vintage beads, lace, ribbon and thread

Fabrics

The main types of vintage fabric to look out for are:

✳ Curtain/upholstery material. This is usually thick and heavy, often floral
   (though 1960s and '70s fabrics can have abstract and even psychedelic
   patterns in very bright colours). It is often linen or heavy cotton.
   These fabrics are not ideal for clothes as they can be very stiff
   so won't hang well on the body. They are of course ideal for
   making your own furnishings and also for bags and other
   items which need strong fabric, although because of age
   and any invisible damage to the fibres, vintage material
   may not be strong enough to withstand heavy use.
   Cotton fabric can usually be washed but may shrink. If
   the fabric includes any special weaves or finishes,
   washing could alter them, so cut a small swatch to
   test. Cotton or synthetic-mix velvet is also common.
   Washing velvet isn't a good idea – it can sometimes
   destroy the pile, although some cotton velvet will wash
   without any problems. Always test a small piece first if you
   are in any doubt. See also p.34 for more information on
   re-using old curtains.

Vintage shot taffeta

49

✳ Dress cottons/other dress fabrics. Lighter-weight fabrics designed for clothes are generally known as dressweight. The older ones are almost always 36in./91.5cm wide or less; to make a full-skirted 1950s dress, four or five yards was needed, so often the pieces you will find for sale are good lengths. Cotton, in good condition, is perfectly washable at least in the first instance. To help preserve it, you should hand wash finished garments.

✳ Rayon and other synthetics. Rayon or 'art silk' (short for artificial) was an exciting fabric developed in the 1930s from plant cellulose and provided a cheap alternative to silk in the 1940s. It often has a crepe look to it and can be very similar to silk but usually feels heavier, more like modern viscose but with a slight sheen. The most common colours for rayon are pale pastel colours used for underwear, particularly a fleshy, peachy pink. Sometimes you can find it in bright, vibrant floral prints, typical of the late 1930s. It is best used for lightly-worn clothes or accessories, rather than bags or anything which is subject to wear and tear, and you should handwash it to be on the safe side. See p.13 for more information on rayon.

✳ Vintage silk. Silk fabrics are quite hard to find because they don't last terribly well. Silks can be plain or printed and some heavier ones may be furnishing fabric. Silk is often attacked by moths so tell-tale holes are a good indicator that the fabric is silk (if it's clearly not wool). Vintage silks were probably originally intended to be dry-cleaned rather than washed. Washing silk can change its feel and texture so if this is important to the particular fabric, then take it to a reputable dry cleaner. I always wash silks anyway, to make sure they harbour no moths, and don't worry about losing the crispness of the fabric. Some silks were (and still are) treated with metallic salts to give them a crispness and weightiness. Because of the chemicals, weighted silks disintegrate more rapidly than untreated silk – this process is called 'shattering' by textile conservators. It is commonly seen in dresses and linings where the fabric splits and shreds. It cannot be repaired, so if silks seem to be starting to shatter, don't bother trying to rescue them. Use silk for gently-used clothes and accessories only, it is not usually strong enough for cushions.

✳ Wool. Coats, skirts and suits were usually made with good quality wool or tweeds until the 1970s so it is often possible to find nice lengths of vintage wool. As with silk, watch out for moths and treat as described on p.53.

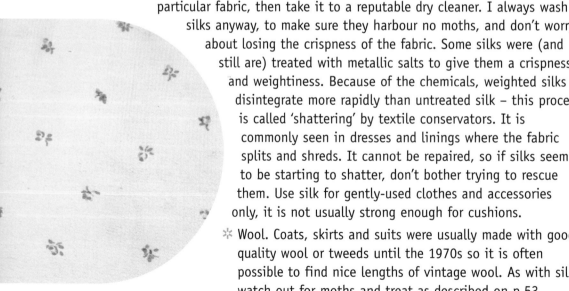

Rayon

Wool will shrink in hot water so if you don't want to dry-clean it, always wash the fabric very gently in cool water and don't wring or rub it or the wool will start to felt. Wool is generally quite hardwearing so can be used for bags, cushions and regularly-worn garments.

* Barkcloth. Despite its name, barkcloth fabric isn't really made of bark, it's simply a slightly waffle-textured linen or cotton fabric, often used for upholstery fabrics in the 1950s. It should be fine to carefully handwash.

* Vintage embroideries. The most common types of embroideries are white linen cloths with colourful embroidery covering pre-printed embroidery designs. These were very popular and they turn up all over the place. They are usually colour fast and can be washed easily either by hand or on a gentle machine cycle. Wash finished pieces by hand.

* Lace. Dressmaking lengths of lace are uncommon but they do turn up from time to time. Always check for tears and damage and always handwash with extreme care, making sure you don't damage the fabric if you are wearing rings. Don't wring and make sure not to stretch it when it's wet. Press dry between two towels. When cutting and sewing lace, try using old bedlinen as backing and cut the two fabrics out at the same time; this stops the lace stretching. Lace or crochet doilies and small cloths are usually quite washable and sturdy as long as they are not damaged or unravelling in the first place.

* Antique fabrics. Anything beaded, with metallic thread, with silk or delicate embroidery should be treated very carefully. Unless it's obviously very dirty, I wouldn't recommend washing anything fragile; simply leave pieces out to air to get rid of musty smells. Don't hang any delicate item on a washing line, always lie it flat. You could try spot cleaning by gentle brushing, using water or even dry-cleaning fluid.

Dating fabrics

It is not always easy to date fabrics but it can be useful to know roughly how old fabrics are and hazarding an educated guess will be easier if you take some time to familiarise yourself with the common styles of each decade of the 20th century. I find the best way learn the types of fabrics from particular eras is to look at the clothes of that decade, in vintage shops, museums and books. You will start to recognise the floral patterns of the 1950s compared to the '30s and learn to spot the type of printed rayon commonly used for 1940s slips. Vintage shops where the clothes are well-identified and dated are fantastic because you can feel the fabrics and learn what rayon or taffeta feels like. Books about fabric design can help you learn the prints and weaves that were most common. Any dressmaking fabric 36in./91.5cm wide or less will probably be pre-1960s, unless it's a later lining or cheap fabric (see p.48).

Haberdashery

I love nothing more than a box of vintage sewing stuff: buttons, lace, ribbons, threads, and pretty packets of needles (why do they never look like that anymore?). By using vintage materials we can reduce the number of new products being made and reduce landfill caused by throwing them away.

I buy spools of secondhand sewing threads whenever I see them and use them in all sorts of sewing projects. Sometimes old threads can become brittle and fragile so won't work well in a sewing machine. But they are usually fine for hand sewing or for tacking, especially if they are on a plastic spool. Wooden spools are of course older so the threads are more likely to be fragile. I tend to keep the very old ones for show.

If you use bias binding, buy old packets in different colours when you see them. Elastic does not last well as it perishes, so isn't worth buying elastic secondhand unless it is new factory waste. Hooks and eyes and poppers haven't changed in years, so as long as they aren't rusty, there's no reason why you shouldn't use them.

Old tins full of gorgeous vintage buttons are one of the vintage sewer's dream finds. We all hope to find the most amazing tin of 1930s buttons in perfect condition. Mostly though, button collections contain a lot of plain and boring plastic buttons with just a few gems hidden underneath. Most buttons are very durable and will cope with being gently washed in water with soap, unless of course they are fabric, or metal which may rust. Plastic, glass and shell can all be washed and scrubbed with an old toothbrush, but watch out for any painted buttons as you might lose the paint along with the dirt. I don't recommend machine washing anything decorated with vintage buttons unless you are absolutely sure they are sturdy enough. Glass buttons are easily damaged and many others will also come out of a machine wash definitely looking worse for wear. Handwash the garment or be prepared to remove the buttons for each wash. Read a book about collectable buttons if you want to find out more, otherwise simply enjoy your finds.

Trimmings

Ribbon, lace, braids and decorative details are wonderful. I keep boxes and boxes of pretty scraps, which I can hunt through to find just the right piece for my next project. You need to have a good stock to find what you need – a perfect excuse to buy up any bags and boxes of trimmings you see at a good price. Coloured ribbons and trims may not be colourfast so test before you attach them to something you would like to wash. Most trimmings won't withstand regular machine washing so treat them carefully.

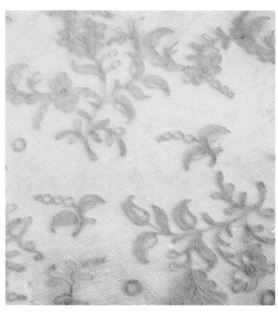

Antique lace

Moths

Be vigilant in your watch for moths, and if you do see any signs isolate the fabric and treat it IMMEDIATELY. Do not risk a moth infestation in your stash; it is soul-destroying. If the fabric is machine washable, put it straight in. If not, try the following method; put the infested item in a large, zip-lock plastic bag and place in the freezer for a few days. Remove the bag from the freezer and let it return to room temperature before opening, then wash the item carefully or brush off the waste material and air the fabric.

Prevention is essential. Where there is any risk of moths, storing fabrics in plastic crates is an excellent idea. Clothes moths attack animal-based fibres like wool, silk and cashmere. Other fibres should be fine, but if there is a serious infestation, keep all fabrics protected and deal with the moth problem by removing all potential foodstuff (including actual food) and vacuum the carpet every day. Natural moth repellents such as lavender and cedarwood may be useful, but if there is an infestation in the house isolating the fabric is the only way to be sure of protecting it, without resorting to chemical mothballs.

Getting rid of the smell of mothballs is difficult, though if fabric has been stored with mothballs you can at least be fairly sure it is moth-free. If you wash the fabric it will just release more of the vile odour. The best advice is to hang the offending fabric or garment on the washing line and leave it there for several days, come rain or shine. If it hasn't had a good rain-wash by this point, handwash the fabric outside and then leave it to dry again. Repeat and repeat until it works. Obviously you can't do this with anything really precious or delicate, so if you have to, take it to the dry-cleaners and see what they can do.

Clothes

Vintage clothes can be treated in the same way as fabrics. The main thing to watch out for is underarm damage. The salt in sweat is destructive to fabric, in the long run, and the underarm area of dresses is often irreparably damaged. You can't easily get rid of the stains and the odour can linger an awfully long time. The fabric can also degrade too. Again there is nothing you can do. If you are planning to re-use the fabrics anyway, then just discard the damaged area.

Storage

However good a condition your vintage fabric is in when you buy it, it will only last well if you treat it kindly. For long-term storage, use museum-quality acid-free boxes and acid-free tissue, and keep the box out of cold or damp places. A bedroom is a good place to store fabrics as the temperature should be fairly constant. Garages are not the place for fabrics and lofts are not ideal either.

When storing fabrics which you are planning to use, I find chests of drawers are best. Air can circulate but the fabrics are protected from light damage and dust. If you have to put fabrics into crates, try wooden boxes, wicker baskets/crates or acid-free cardboard boxes rather than plastic, to allow air to circulate. Cover the top with old sheets to protect from dust or pets. If you have to store fabrics in a potentially damp or dusty room, or in moth-risk areas, store them in sealed plastic crates. Put damp-absorbing silica gel sachets inside to keep the fabrics dry. Check regularly and air the fabrics

Vintage sewing kit

every few months. If you have the space, fabrics always look lovely folded neatly and stacked on shelves, and this also allows you to browse and select easily, and to arrange your fabrics by type or colour. This is ideal if you use lots of different fabrics regularly (for making quilts, for example) but not so useful if you are a one-project-at-a-time person. If there is strong sunlight in the room, use blinds or cover your fabrics with old sheets to protect them.

'Little Betty' child's sewing machine

DAMAGE

Before you buy vintage fabric, unfold it, hold it up to good light and use the following list to check for potential problems:

- Stains
- Tears and holes
- Splits, particularly on fold lines
- Insect damage (mainly in silk and wool)
- Mothball smell (you can't miss it!)
- Light damage, usually fading, although sometimes the colour is fast but the fabric has been irreversibly damaged by light exposure. Light damage usually degrades the fibres so the fabric appears to be disintegrating.
- Water marks – where water has left a stain on the fabric. This can sometimes wash out but don't count on it.
- Rust marks (these are usually irreversible)
- Silk shatter. See p.50.
- Depending on the fabric, what you want to use it for, and the price, you may not care too much about any of these things. If you only want to use small bits then you can work around most damage. If you want to make a dress using a lot of the fabric then you should avoid anything with large areas of damage, particularly fold lines.

5 Basic sewing: tools and techniques

All the sewing projects in this book require a basic sewing kit. Many of the projects do not necessarily require a sewing machine and remember it is possible to make anything by hand, although it might take a while to finish sewing a skirt or handbag. It would be very eco to sew without an electric machine, but, being realistic, few of us have the time or the inclination to hand sew everything.

HAND SEWING KIT

* A range of **hand-sewing needles**. The most useful ones are called Sharps and you will find a mixed pack of sizes 5-10 best.

* **Thread.** Threads are usually polyester, cotton or a mixture. Either is usually fine. Polyester is stronger and is recommended in certain projects. Always buy good quality thread, as cheap thread tends to break. Organic cotton sewing threads are now available in the US.

* **Fabric scissors.** Large, sharp fabric scissors are essential and worth spending money on.

* **Small scissors.** A medium-sized pair is useful for small projects. Tiny embroidery or nail scissors with sharp points are good for unpicking and clipping threads.

* **Measuring tape.** A plastic or fabric measuring tape is essential for large projects or dressmaking. A 30cm/12in.-ruler is also useful.

* **Pins.** Longer, finer pins (called lace or dressmakers' pins) are better than cheap, short ones. Pins with coloured glass heads are easier to use; plastic heads can melt on contact with the iron.

* **Iron & pressing cloth**. A good steam iron is essential for all sewing projects. A pressing cloth is simply a protective cloth to put between the iron and the fabric you are pressing. A clean tea towel or linen napkin works fine.

MACHINE SEWING KIT

You will need everything in the hand sewing kit (opposite) as well as the following items.

✳ **Sewing machine**. There is no need for a brand-new machine; a re-conditioned machine can work for decades and it is far more eco to use an old one than to buy new. A good sewing machine shop will advise you on which type of second-hand machine would best suit your needs. Start with a basic machine and upgrade if you find you are sewing a lot and require a greater number of functions. The most essential functions are reverse (to secure threads at the start and end), straight stitch and zigzag stitch. An automatic buttonhole function is very useful if you want to make clothes.

✳ **Machine needles**. There are different thicknesses and types of needles available for standard sewing machines. Fine or delicate fabrics should be sewn with size 60 or 70 fine needles while size 80 is the standard size suitable for most fabrics. Jeans and thick upholstery fabrics should be sewn with size 90 or 100. Ballpoint needles are for jersey fabrics. Other needles are available for different purposes such as machine embroidery. Always change the needle if it catches in your fabric or if you have run over a pin – a damaged needle may cause problems stitching, and may cut your thread or snag the fabric. This is particularly important when sewing fine or delicate fabrics.

Stitches

Running stitch

Running stitch is used to join two pieces of fabric together. It is not secure so it is best used for temporary stitching (basting or tacking) and for decorative top-stitching.

To make the stitch, secure the thread with two small stitches or a knot. Bring the needle in and out of the fabric at 3-6mm intervals.

Backstitch

Backstitch is used to make firm and permanent seams. It can be used in place of machine sewing.

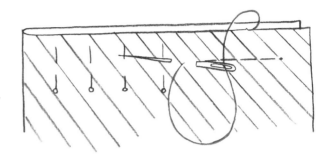

To make backstitch, first knot the thread or make two small stitches to secure the thread. Stitch into the fabric, bringing the needle out about 5mm further along past where the thread goes in.

Slip stitch

Slip stitch is a quick and easy hand stitch for joining two pieces together. It can be used to sew hems, close openings and attach appliqué.

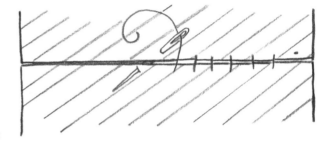

Starting in the upper fabric, bring the needle underneath the fabric and diagonally down to pick up just a few threads from the lower fabric. Then pick up a few threads from the upper fabric and repeat. Keep the stitches small and neat and it will be nearly invisible.

Hems

Hems are used on the sides and bottoms of garments or other projects to finish the raw edge.

Single hem

A single hem is quick and easy but the raw edge needs finishing before you start or it will fray. Single hems are often used in factory-made clothing with the edge finished on an overlocker sewing machine. This technique can be used to repair ready-made hems that are coming unstitched.

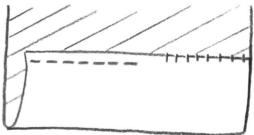

First, finish the raw edge if required by using pinking shears, zig zag stitching or hand overcasting. Fold the fabric along the hemline and press. Sew the hem using a machine, with medium-length stitches (left) or by hand, using slip stitch (right).

Double hem

In a double hem, the raw edge is enclosed so you do not need to finish the edge. It makes a more bulky seam, so may not be ideal for thick fabrics.

Fold over about 1cm/⅓in. and press. Fold again at the hemline and press. Sew by hand or machine as above.

Seams

Seams are where two pieces of fabric are joined together by stitching. There are many different types of seam, which you can find in specialist sewing manuals. This basic seam will work for all the projects in this book.

To make a simple seam, place the two pieces of fabric face to face and match the raw edges together. Mark the seamline (usually 1.5cm/⅝in. from the raw edge) with tailors' chalk. Pin in place and tack if the fabric is slippery. Sew along the marked seam line. If using a sewing machine, check the throat plate of the machine for little marks – the 1.5cm/⅝in. mark will show you where to place the raw edge of your fabric to sew along this seam allowance.

To turn a corner, sew up to 1.5cm/⅝in. from the edge, then stop and turn the wheel so the needle is down in the fabric. Lift up the presser foot and rotate the fabric using the needle as a pivot, then put the presser foot down again and continue sewing.

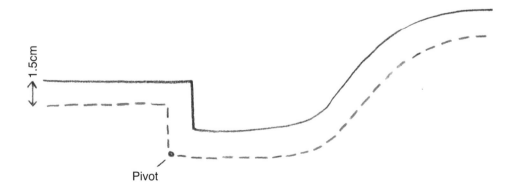

Pivot

Pressing and finishing seam allowances

From the inside, open out the seam and press the seam allowances open. The raw edges can be finished with zigzag stitching or hand overcasting to stop the fraying. Cutting with pinking shears will also prevent some fabrics from fraying a lot. You can finish the raw edges before you sew the seam, if you prefer.

Zigzagging the two seam allowances together is fast and easy but leaves a bulky seam that will show through when you iron the finished garment. It's fine for cushions and handbags, but not ideal for items where the seam will be opened out, such as the skirt on p.128.

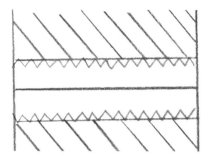

Some seams can be very bulky and should be trimmed so they sit flat and to avoid ridges on the outside. Trim away a small amount of the seam allowance, cutting each layer separately and at different heights, so the seam allowances are layered. Don't cut any closer than 5mm from stitching. Don't trim fabrics that fray a lot – finish the edges as above.

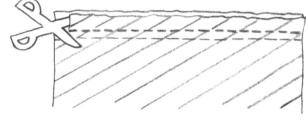

Curved seams must be shaped to make them lie flat when they are ironed. Inward curves should be clipped so the fabric can spread out. Outward curves need to have little V-shaped notches cut into them. Use small, sharp scissors to cut into the seam allowance, but never cut too close to the stitching or the seam can tear.

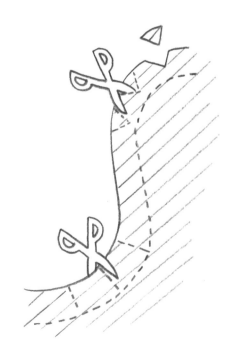

Zips

There are several methods for inserting zips, but this quick and simple method works fine for the projects in this book.

Shortening a zip

Measure the length required from the top. Mark where the zip should end and sew over the teeth at the marked point using close zigzag stitching or stitch across the teeth by hand. Cut through the zip 2cm/¾in. below the stitching, being very careful with metal zip teeth.

Basic zip

First sew the main seam up to the bottom of the zip placement. Hand tack the remaining seam closed using large running stitch. Press the seam allowance open.

1. Check the zip placement on the pattern. Place the zip teeth-side down on the seam, lining up the top of the tape with the top edge of the fabric and the teeth along the seam line. Fold the zip pull tag so it sticks up.

2. Pin and tack the zip in place using running stitch. Remove the pins.

3. Sew from the front, either by hand or by machine (using a zip foot so you can sew close to the teeth). Starting at the top, sew down one side to the bottom then pivot 90° at the corner (see p.59), sew across the zip, pivot 90° again and sew back up the other side. Keep the stitching line straight and make sure you are sewing through all the layers including the zip tape.

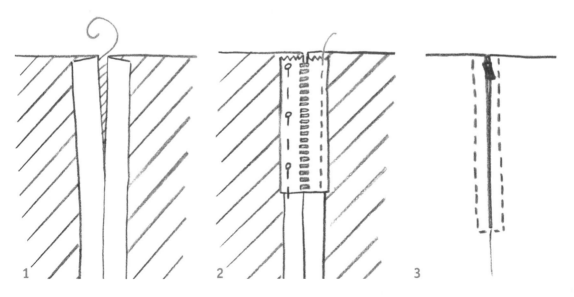

If it is difficult to sew around the zip pull, leave the needle in the fabric, lift the presser foot and unzip. Then put the presser foot back down and continue sewing.

When complete, remove all the tacking threads.

NB: A zip foot is a narrow foot that allows you to sew close to the zip teeth without the presser foot getting in the way. Some machines allow you move the needle to one side to stitch even closer to the zip teeth. Check the manual to see if yours will do this.

Pressing and ironing

In sewing books you will see the term pressing, rather than ironing. This is almost the same thing, but not quite. Ironing is for getting creases out of clothes and involves moving the iron around. Pressing is for flattening fabric prior to or after sewing, and for opening seam allowances and setting shapes. It is very much as it sounds – pressing down with the iron, rather than moving it around. Keeping the iron still stops seam allowances or interfacing etc from sliding around. It is best to use a pressing cloth, especially for any delicate fabrics; a clean tea towel or linen napkin works perfectly well.

6 Home projects

Pincushion

Pincushions are great things to make using new techniques or materials and are perfect for using up small scraps. They are also excellent gifts for new or seasoned sewers. The simple leaf appliqué has been embellished by attaching vintage or decorative buttons using pins with coloured heads.

Materials

- Plain fabric (organic cotton in this sample) One piece 23x17cm/9x7in. for front panel. Two pieces each 17x13cm/7x5in. for the back.
- Scrap of wool felt about 15x20cm/6x8in. (see pp.38-9). To cut out a detailed leaf shape, thin wool felt is best. It is harder to cut details in a very thick felt.
- Photocopier paper wrapper or freezer paper
- Fabric scraps or raw wool for stuffing. You can use sawdust as long as the main fabric you use is a very close weave and the sawdust will not leak out.

Equipment

- Leaf template (right)

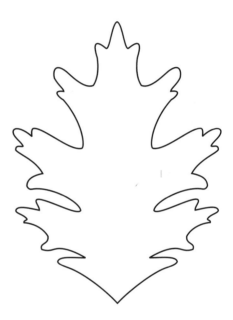

Pincushion motif @ 50%

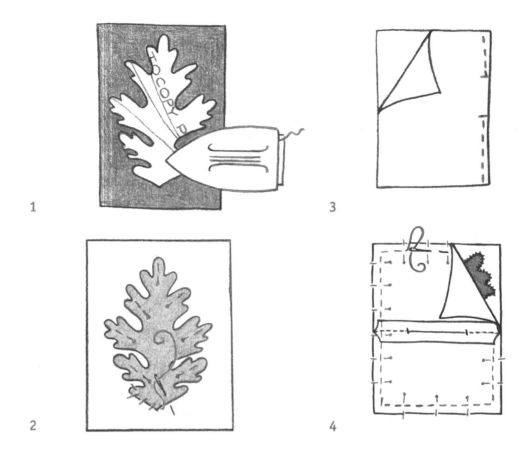

1

2

3

4

1. First create a leaf template by enlarging the template on p.64 by 200% or by drawing around a real leaf. Trace the leaf shape onto the non-shiny side of the wrapper or freezer paper and cut out using paper scissors. Press the wool felt so it has no creases. Place the freezer paper leaf shiny-side DOWN onto the wool felt. Press briefly with a warm iron. Check that the template has stuck.

2. Cut out the wool shape, following the edge of the template. This is easier to do with small, sharp scissors. Do not peel off the paper until you are ready to sew the felt leaf on. Position the leaf in the centre of

the front fabric piece, not too close to the edges. Pin in place. Using a matching thread and fastening on the underside, sew all around the leaf shape using small slipstitches (see p.58).

3. Join the two back panel pieces along the long sides using 1.5cm/⅝in. seam allowance, leaving a 5cm/2in. gap in the middle. Press the seam allowance open.

4. Place the appliquéd front panel face up, and the back panel face down (so the seam allowances face towards you). Pin, then sew all round the pincushion, with 1.5cm/⅝in. seam allowances.

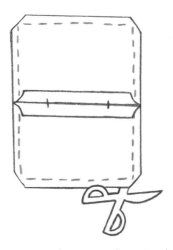

5

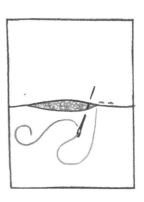

6

5. Clip the corners (not too close to the stitching) then turn the pincushion the right way out, using a knitting needle to turn out the corners. Press flat.

6. Stuff with tiny fabric scraps, raw wool or sawdust. Sew up the hole in the back seam using slipstitch. Decorate the pincushion using coloured-head pins and buttons.

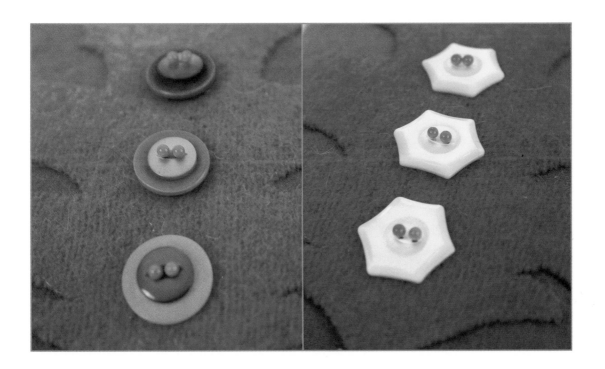

Chair seat cover

Refurbishing a dining chair with a patchwork seat cover is a great project for using up scraps of co-ordinating fabric. This project is designed for a drop-in seat and would also work for a screw-on seat. If the chair you plan to use has cut out corners, refer to an upholstery book for more information on how to cover this type of seat. The instructions below explain how to make the fabric cover for a well-upholstered seat, but not how to re-upholster the seat as well. The chair I started with had a badly collapsed seat and needed reupholstery. If this is the case with your chair, start by reviving the seat before you make the fabric cover.

You have a few options:

* Take it to any upholsterer. Modern, economy upholstery often makes use of foams, glues and treatments involving potentially harmful chemicals. You may prefer to look for an upholsterer who will use traditional and more natural materials such as horsehair and wool.
* Take it to an eco-upholsterer who will use fewer chemicals. An organic upholsterer is recommended in the resources section.
* Learn upholstery yourself. Many colleges run evening and weekend courses in upholstery and a drop-in seat is an ideal first project. Bear in mind the issues of chemical use if that bothers you and do your research to find a course where you can use more natural materials.
* Get a book out of the library on traditional upholstery, track down the necessary resources online or through local phone books and re-upholster the seat yourself.

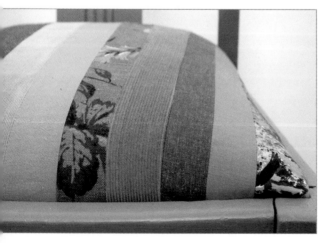

If the seat itself is in good condition, but just needs a little extra padding, try using quilt wadding in layers over the seat. You could try organic cotton or wool, rather than polyester or foam which is normally recommended.

Once you have a seat ready to cover, this project is very quick to complete.

Chair seat detail

Materials

- Scraps of strong, reasonably heavy fabric, such as upholstery or curtain fabrics
- Large sheet of paper – newspaper will do fine – tape two pieces together if necessary
- Piece of scrap fabric twice the size of your chair seat

Equipment

- Pliers to remove nails
- Staple gun or small tacks and hammer
- Machine sewing kit

1. First create the pattern for your own chair seat. On the large sheet of paper, draw around the seat outline and add at least 15cm/6in. all round, or more if your seat is very thick/deep. Cut out the pattern in scrap fabric and test to see if it will fit over the seat and allow plenty on the underside to fasten down.

2. Cut strips of co-ordinating fabrics 6cm/2½in. wide and about 60cm/24in. long (or about 10cm/4in. longer than your pattern). Arrange the strips into a pleasing design and sew together, one at a time, using 1.5cm/⅝in. seam allowances. Press each seam allowance open before you add the next strip. Keep joining until the panel is large enough to accommodate the paper pattern.

3. Press the patchwork panel again from the front then lay wrong-side up. Pin on the pattern and draw around it with chalk. Cut out. Fold the fabric panel into quarters and mark the centre of each side with chalk or a notch.

4. Measure and mark the centre of each side of the drop-in seat. Stretch the fabric over the chair seat, making sure the centre points on the fabric and seat match. This helps to keep the straight lines looking straight! Put a nail or staple LOOSELY in the centre back, then pull the fabric taut and put a LOOSE staple in the centre front. Turn the seat over and check that the fabric looks straight and neat before you hammer the nails or staples in more fully. Take them out and try again if its too wonky.

5. Do the same on each side, making sure the fabric is taut and straight. Then work along the back and front, smoothing the fabric and getting any twists and wrinkles out, then the sides.

6. Finally make the corners. Make neat folds in the corners. Trim away some of the excess fabric if necessary (otherwise the seat may be too thick to fit back into the chair frame). Staple or nail the corners in place and test the seat in the chair frame. Trim any additional excess material then put the seat back into the chair frame. Whack firmly if it is a drop-in seat or screw in place if that is how it attaches.

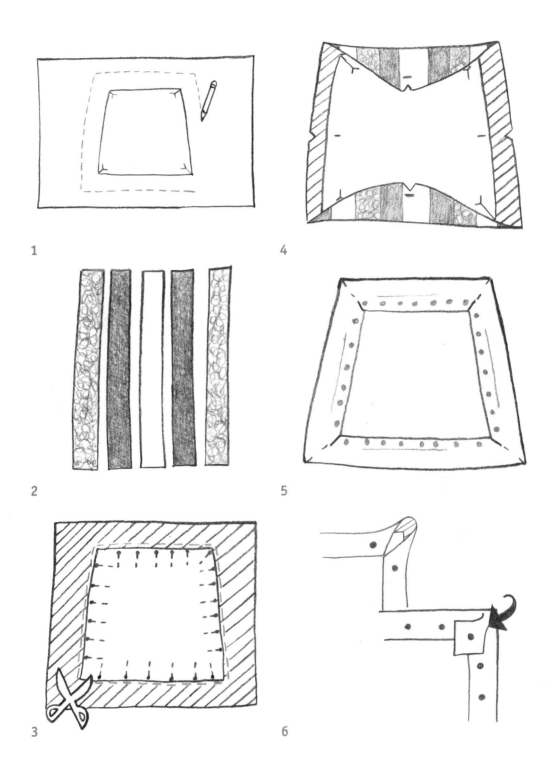

1

2

3

4

5

6

Curtains

If you have plain, boring curtains you can easily transform them with a spectacular frill. It is fiddly but not difficult.

Materials

- One plain curtain
- One large piece of co-ordinating fabric, not too thick. Old duvet covers or sheets work well.
- Good quality polyester thread

Equipment

- Machine sewing kit
- Hand sewing kit

1. First make the ruffle. Cut and join lengths of fabric 35cm/14in. wide to make one piece three times as wide as the curtain. For example, if the curtain is 1.5m/60in. wide, you will need 4.5m/5 yards of fabric 35cm/14in. wide.

2. There are three ways to gather the edges:

a. Machine sew using strong polyester thread and the longest stitch setting. Secure both ends firmly. Use a pin to pull up the top thread every 30cm/12in. or so, and pull through to gather up the fabric. Cut the resulting loop of thread and tie the two ends together firmly so the gathers can't come undone.

b. Hand sew all along the edge and pull up the gathers. As the piece of fabric is so long, this can be really tiresome and the long threads will get tangled. Start sewing without cutting the thread from the spool, and just unwind more as you need it. When you get to the end, sew in the thread then go back to the start, cut the thread, thread it on to a needle and sew in.

c. Use a ruffler or gathering foot if you have one. Gather both sides evenly, making sure the finished ruffle is about

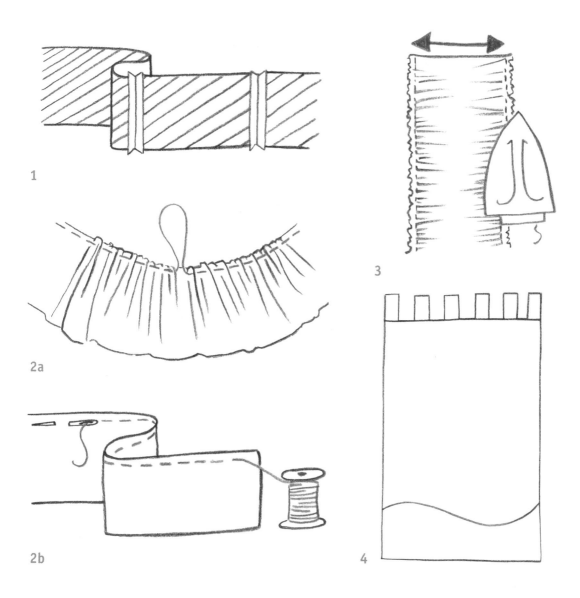

1

2a

2b

3

4

20cm/8in. wider than the curtain. Check the length before you fasten off the threads. Ease out the gathers if it is too narrow, or pull them up more if it is too long.

3. Stretch the ruffle width-ways and iron the edges.

4. Using chalk or soap mark the frill placement on the curtains by drawing the bottom line snaking across in VERY gentle curves.

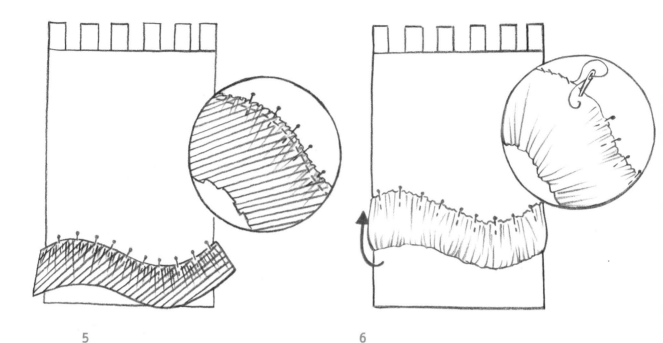

5

6

5. With the curtain laid out flat, right-side up, position the ruffle right side DOWN, facing down, with the edge matching the bottom line marking. Pin in place. Make sure the curtain isn't puckered anywhere. Machine sew along the ruffle, following the line of the gathering stitches.

6. Fold the ruffle up so it faces right side up. Flatten and arrange the ruffle so it sits nicely. Pull up or loosen the gathers where required to make it curve nicely. Tighten the gathers for an inward curve and loosen them for an outward curve. Pin in place.

Hang the curtain up temporarily to make sure it doesn't pucker. Hand sew the top edge of the ruffle in place, turning under the raw edge as you go. Set the ruffle and make the curtain hang better by steaming it once you have hung it up. You can use an ordinary steam iron as long as it has a 'shot of steam' button. Hold the iron 5cm/2in. away from the curtain and blast each area of the ruffle with steam. Make sure you don't scald yourself or drip water onto the carpet. Rubber gloves and newspaper on the floor will help.

Tea cosy

Recycled wool felt makes a lovely, tactile and warm tea cosy. This is just the right size for a medium-large teapot, and easily adjustable to different sizes by enlarging the pattern to suit your pot.

Materials

- One felted jumper, plain or stripy, not too thick (see p.38)
- Scraps of contrasting wool felt (not too thick) or you could use the remaining fabric from the same jumper for an all-matching tea cosy

Equipment

- Machine sewing kit
- Templates for the main body and for the scales on p.79. Note: Enlarge the pattern by 200% or to suit your own tea pot.

*1.5cm/⅝in. seam allowances are included in the pattern pieces.

1. Cut two pieces using the template for the front and back. You can use the jumper ribbing if you want or you can cut the pieces from the main body of the jumper or the opened-out sleeves.

You can resize the template to suit your teapot, but remember you will need more scales for a bigger one, and less for a smaller one. Cut 12 scales from contrasting wool felt.

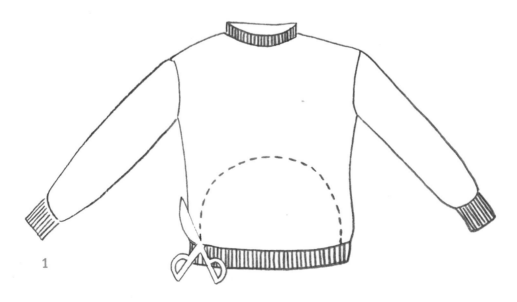

1

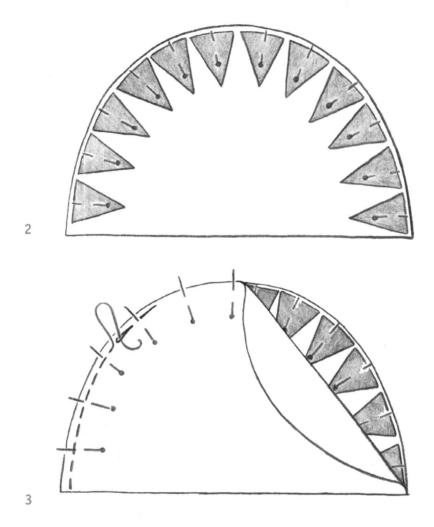

2

3

2. Pin the scales onto one piece of the main body, starting at the centre top (this ensures your scales are evenly arranged across the whole piece). Match up the edges and have the points facing inwards. If the felt has a right side and wrong side, then pin the scales to the right side. You can tack the scales in place and remove the pins if you prefer.

3. Pin the other main body piece on top, pinning between the scales. Using a sewing machine, sew around the curved edge of the tea cosy. As the three layers of felt can be very thick, you will need large stitches and may need to reduce the presser foot pressure if your machine does this. Go slowly. Reverse stitch at the start and end of the sewing. Hand sew if you find it easier with thick layers. Turn the tea cosy the right way out. You don't need to clip the seam allowance.

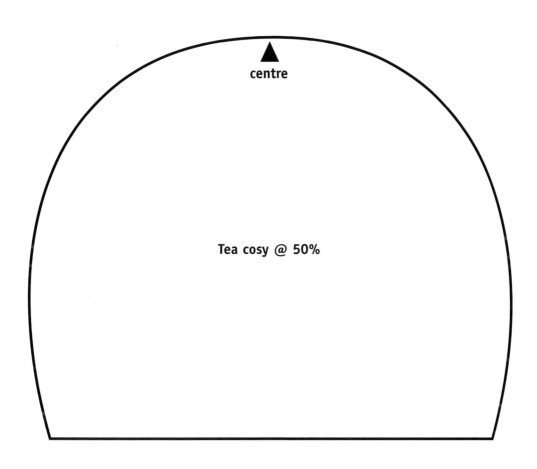

centre

Tea cosy @ 50%

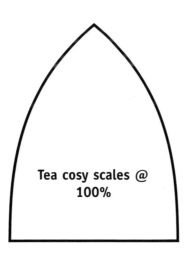

Tea cosy scales @ 100%

Lampshade

This is a really simple way to dress up a plain lampshade. It is easiest to do this on a straight-sided drum shade, or one with gently tapering sides. Only use this lampshade with low-energy bulbs.

Materials

- Lampshade
- Vintage lace

Equipment

- Hand sewing kit
- Thread to match the lace
- Fabric glue (optional)

1. Experiment with the lace to work out how much you need to go around the lampshade. My lace was very wide, but if yours is narrower, you will need to sew several lengths together to make a piece wide enough to cover the whole lampshade. Hand sew the lace together carefully using matching thread. Use small slip stitches (p.58) and make sure not to pucker the lace.

2. Stretch the lace piece around the lampshade, overlap the ends and pin together fairly tightly (with the pins in the lace, not through the lampshade).

3. With the lace still on the lampshade, hand sew the lace to itself using small neat stitches, following the edges of the motifs. Cut away the excess lace about 5mm/¼in. from the stitching.

4. If the lace slides and droops, sew around the top edge of the lace through the lampshade itself, again with small neat stitches. Use a medium-large needle and stab stitch from the outside to the inside, one stitch at a time. If the lampshade is plastic, then all the needle holes will be permanent, so be careful. You can also use glue to hold the lace in place, if you don't want to stitch through the lampshade. Fold back the top edge of the lace and put a fine line of fabric glue on the shade. Leave it to dry clear, then press the lace onto the glue.

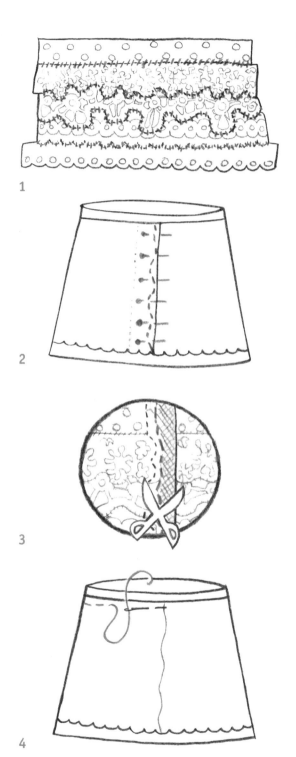

1

2

3

4

Laptop cosy

Recycled jumpers make lovely thick felt ideal for protecting gadgets. The sizes given here are for a small laptop (28x23cm/11x9in.). If you have a larger laptop then use the largest jumper you can find, or piece the panels together from two jumpers. Make the panels 5cm/2in. wider than your laptop and allow extra length in the long panels to make sure it will wrap all the way around. Make a test pattern in paper and allow a little extra length to make up for the thickness of the wool felt.

1. From the jumper cut pieces:
• Two pieces each 33x53cm/13x21in. including the ribbing (use the front and the back for these).
• One piece 23x33cm/9x13in. (use a sleeve for this).

2. Join the small piece to one of the long pieces (at the cut end, not the ribbing end) to make a panel about 75cm/30in. long. Overlap the two pieces and sew through both layers. Use zigzag stitch if the felt stretches. If the felt is too thick to sew easily, you can make a butted seam by putting both raw edges together and using a large zigzag stitch across the seam.

Materials

• 1 large felted jumper (see pp.38-9) – it should be well-felted and quite thick and firm, so it doesn't stretch much. You may need two to get enough fabric for a large laptop.
• 2.5m/98in. ribbon (about 1cm/½in. wide)

Equipment

• Hand sewing kit
• Machine sewing kit

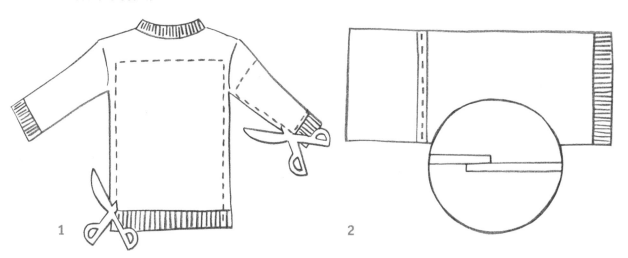

1

2

3. On the right side (outside of jumper) cover the seam with ribbon. Position the ribbon over the seam stitching and turn the ends under. Pin in place and carefully sew all around the edges.

4. The other piece forms the inner pocket. Fold this so the ribbing is on top and the underside extends by 7cm/3in. Tack the sides together.

5. Position the pocket in the middle of the long wrap piece (which should be WRONG side up) with the fold 3cm/1½in. to the right of the seam. Tack into position by hand where the red stitching is shown in the illustration. Test the fit by slipping the laptop into the pocket and folding the unribbed flap over first, then bringing the ribbed flap over the top. If it all fits fine, then machine sew following the tacking stitches. If not, undo the tacking, adjust and repeat the steps to sew the pocket down.

6. Now make the ribbon ties. Cut the remaining ribbon into two 30cm/12in. lengths (this is for the top flap) and two 60cm/23in. lengths for the bottom flap. Finish the ends of the ribbon turning the end over twice and handsewing down. The longer ribbons go on the underneath (unribbed) flap. Position the ribbon on the right side of the fabric, extending away from the flap, 8cm/3in. from the outside edge (as shown in the photo). Turn the end under and pin in place. Machine sew in a neat square around the folded end of the ribbon. Repeat on the top flap (ribbed part). Finally make the holes to thread the ribbon through. The holes are in the front flap, right next to the edge of the

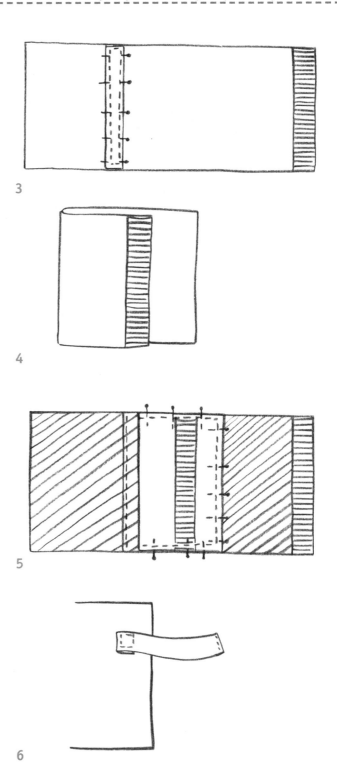

3

4

5

6

extension, where it is sewn down. Mark the position of the holes 8cm/3in. in from the edge. Make a tiny snip into the felt at the marked position. You will not need to cut any more of a hole and the edges will not fray.

Put the laptop into the pocket and the fold the underflap over, passing the ribbons through the holes. Bring the top flap over and bring the ribbons underneath to tie together.

You will find you have a secret pocket beneath the laptop pocket. Use it to keep secret bits and pieces in.

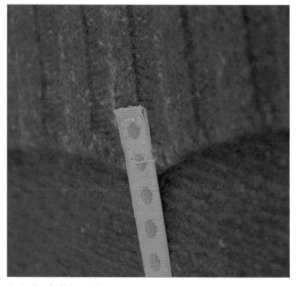

Detail of ribbon tie

Suede cushion

Suede skirts often turn up in charity shops and can be re-purposed into wonderfully luxurious cushions. The great thing about suede is that it doesn't fray, so you can cut detailed designs in it. A leather skirt would also work.

Materials

- One suede skirt for the front panel
- One large shirt for the back and lining
- Cushion inner – either readymade or make your own (see p.42)
- Polyester thread (it lasts longer than cotton when used with leather or suede)

Equipment

- Machine sewing kit
- Masking tape
- Craft knife and cutting mat
- Leather needle for sewing machine
- Cut-out template on p.87, or design your own
- Variable-size leather punch (optional)

Note on cushion size: Bear in mind the size of cushion filler you will need. The skirt you use may not yield enough fabric for a standard-size (40cm/16in.) cushion inner. You may be able to get a smaller one and then work to the right size. If you are going to make your own cushion inner then make the suede cushion to the maximum size you can, and make an inner exactly the right dimensions to fit.

1. Cut up the side seams of the skirt and select the front or back to use for the cushion. Work out the maximum size square or rectangle you can get from the skirt panel and cut it out. Sharp sewing scissors will work fine. If the suede is creased, iron it on low heat with baking paper on top to protect it. Do not use steam.

2. Photocopy or trace the template onto thin card. Use a sharp knife and a cutting mat to cut out the design along the black lines. Use a leather punch or a paper punch to cut the circles.

3. Decide upon the placement of the design on your suede panel, ensuring it will sit at least 7-10cm/3-4in. in from any edge. Turn the suede over and tape the template in position on the back of the suede panel. Draw through the cut-out design using a felt tip or ballpoint pen. Remove the template. Put the suede on the cutting mat and carefully cut the design using a very sharp blade. Hold the suede carefully with one hand while you

cut, to stop it sliding and stretching. If you have a leather punch, use this to cut the circles. Otherwise cut them by hand using small pointed scissors.

4. Cut the shirt into flat pieces by cutting along the side seams, around the armholes and across the shoulders. Using the front only, cut a panel the same size as your suede panel with the buttons in the middle. Cut a panel the same size from the shirt back to make the lining of the suede front. Place the button piece face up, the suede face down on top of it, and the back of the shirt piece face down on top. Remove any buttons from the seam allowance. DON'T PIN!

You can't pin through suede, so use mini pegs or paperclips to hold all the edges in place. Stitch holes will be permanent, so make sure you are absolutely correct before you sew. Sew around the cushion using 1.5cm/⅝in. seam allowances. If the layers of fabric are too thick to go through the machine, reduce the presser foot pressure if you can. The suede is sandwiched between the layers of fabric so it should be trouble-free to sew. Turn out and press the corners under baking paper as before.

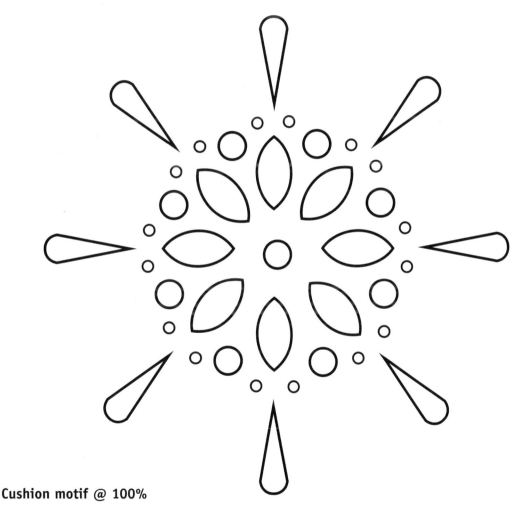

Cushion motif @ 100%

Apron

This apron is my solution to the problem of what to do with a lovely skirt which doesn't fit but you can't bear to get rid of. Printed, patterned and embroidered skirts often turn up in charity shops, all too often in the wrong sizes. It would also work with a vintage skirt that has lots of fabric in the skirt but is too small in the waist. Transform the never-worn skirt into an apron instead – one size fits all.

This skirt is best made from a lightweight, fairly floaty fabric – a thin cotton or even silk is good, or viscose. If you want your apron to be washable (which would be sensible) then pre-wash the skirt first, to get any shrinkage over with before you start. Use a skirt with as few panels as possible, as lots of seams will stop the apron from hanging nicely.

Materials
- Skirt
- 10cm/4in. of 150cm/55in.-wide fabric or 20cm/8in. of narrower-width fabric or enough to make strips for a waistband 10cm wide by 150-200cm/55-80in. long

Equipment
- Hand sewing kit
- Machine sewing kit

The skirt, before deconstructing

1. Deconstruct the skirt by unpicking the waistband and fastenings. You need to then unpick either the back seam or one of the side seams to open up the skirt into one long panel. It depends on the design on your skirt. For this one, I opened the side seam where the zip was because that made the design symmetrical. If you open up a different seam to where you have taken out the zip, sew up the zip seam instead. Leave the hem unless you want to shorten the apron, in which case you will need to sew the hem. Unpick any darts or pleats in the skirt. Press any creases out and neaten up the top raw edge.

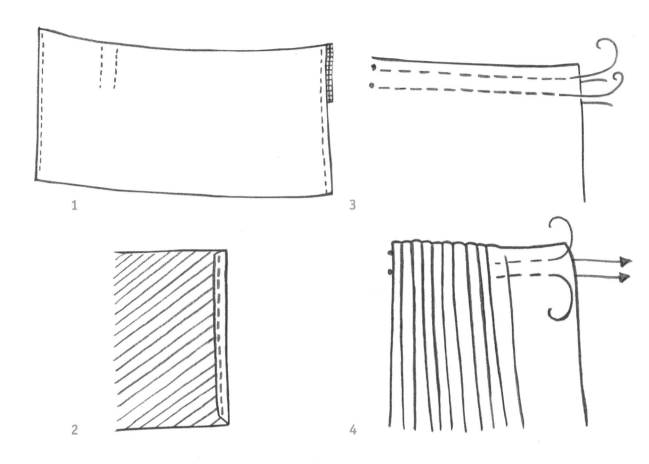

1

2

3

4

2. Hem the side seams using a narrow double hem (see p.59).

3. Mark a line with vanishing pen or chalk 1.5cm/⅝in. down from the top raw edge. With a long stitch, machine sew along the line. Fasten the threads firmly at the start with a couple of backstitches but at the end leave the threads long and unfastened. Repeat this 2cm below the first stitched line and again 2cm below that so you have three rows of gathering.

4. Take hold of the long threads left at the end, and pull just on the bobbin threads. The fabric will start to gather. Pull very gently and slide the gathers along the threads to the fastened end (this is why it is important to fasten the threads at the start, or the gathers will just slide straight off the end). Keep gently pulling up the threads and sliding the gathers down, bit by bit, until the gathered fabric is about 30-40cm/12-16in. wide. Hold the apron up to your waist to see if you want it more or less gathered. When the width is right, tie the long threads firmly together, trim to a manageable length and hand stitch the threads down to fasten them neatly in the side hem. You can sew the gathering stitches by hand if you don't have a machine; just make 5-8mm/¼-½in. running stitches.

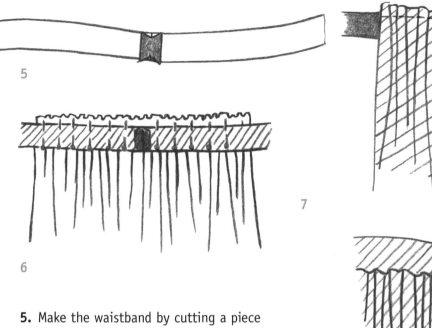

5

6

7

8

9

5. Make the waistband by cutting a piece of fabric 10cm/4in. wide and 150-200cm/55-80in. long. If necessary, make the waistband using two or even three pieces sewn together; just make sure the seam allowances are pressed open. If you aren't sure how long to make the waistband and ties, test with some ribbon to see what length is comfortable.

6. Mark the centre of the waistband strip. Measure and mark the centre of the gathered apron. Match the centre of the waistband to the centre of the skirt, making sure the seams are facing up (so the waistband and apron are right sides together). Pin in place then turn over.

7. With the apron facing right-side up, sew through the apron and waistband, following the first row of gathering stitches. This will leave the lower two rows of stitching showing under the finished waistband creating a smocked effect.

8. Fold the waistband up. Press the seam allowance under along the remaining unsewn waistband edge. Press the seam allowance up all along the other long edge of the waistband.

9. Fold the ends of the waistband in half, right sides together. At each end, sew diagonally from the corner on the fold to the two folded edges.

10

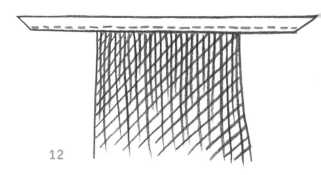

12

11

10. Trim away the excess fabric, leaving about 5mm/¼in.

11. Turn out the pointed end of the waistbands and fold back the right way out, making sure the seam allowances are tucked inside. Press flat.

12. Pin the waistband together and sew all along the open edge, over the apron (enclosing the raw edge) and to the other pointed end.

Detail of the waistband

Tablelinen

Appliqué is an easy way to completely transform a plain, vintage tablecloth into something contemporary and stylish, and at the same time cover up any stains! You could also use a vintage linen or heavy cotton sheet – I used an embroidered Swiss cotton sheet which was in perfect condition and wonderfully heavy. If you want to start with new fabric, organic cotton sheeting is ideal – it is extra wide, 2.85m/112in., so you can easily buy a piece big enough for even the largest dining table.

Materials

- Large piece of organic cotton, vintage tablecloth or vintage sheet
- Scraps of medium-weight, washable fabrics which don't fray too much
- Embroidery threads

Note: You may prefer to iron lightweight interfacing onto the fabric scraps before cutting them out. It stops the fabrics from fraying and wrinkling. See p.40 for more information about interfacing.

Equipment

- Hand sewing kit
- Safety pins
- Items to use as circle templates – plates, jars, CDs

1. Pre-wash the base fabric and all the scraps you use for this project as you don't want colours running in the wash. Also use a dye grabber when you wash, to catch any excess (see p.38). Wash and iron the tablecloth/sheet/fabric. Mark any stains with safety pins so you can easily find them to cover with appliqué. If you are using new fabric, cut to the required size and hem all the edges.

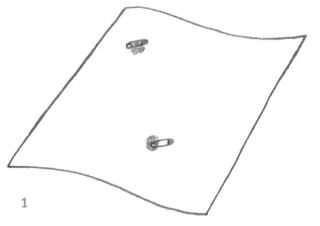

1

2. Cut circles from medium-weight fabrics in a range of different sizes, from 6-20cm/2½-8in. I used about 60 for this project. Spread out the cloth and pin the circles in a nice arrangement over the cloth, covering any stains if necessary. Pin in place, again using safety pins.

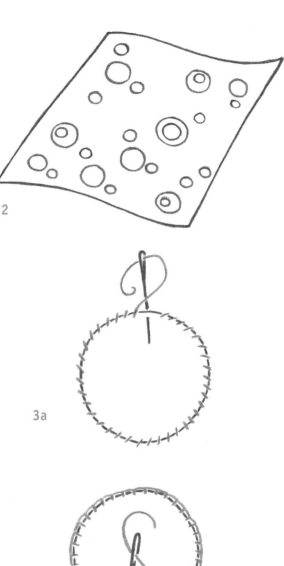

2

3. Starting at one side of the cloth, sew the circles down. Sew around the edges of each circle using either slipstitch (**a**) or blanket stitch (**b**). Slipstitch is much faster, so it depends how long you are prepared to work on the tablecloth! Tack or use more pins if required and smooth out each circle to ensure it doesn't wrinkle as you sew. Press when all the appliqués are attached.

It is quick and easy to make vintage linen napkins to match by sewing just a few small circles onto one corner of each napkin.

3a

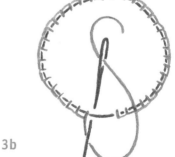

3b

Napkin

Slashed cushion

This cushion is a great way to recycled either beloved old clothes or just nice things you have found in the charity shop. For this project you need to start with an unfelted jumper.

Bear in mind the size of cushion filler you will need. A standard size jumper will shrink and only make a cushion of about 35cm/14in. max. If you want to use a ready-made cushion inner, then cut the felted wool to the right size. If you are going to make your own cushion inner then make the felted cushion to the maximum size you can, and make an inner exactly the right dimensions to fit (see p.42).

Materials
- 1 wool jumper suitable for felting, largest size possible (see pp.38-9)
- 1 contrasting men's cotton shirt
- Cushion inner made to required size

Equipment
- Machine sewing kit
- Rotary cutter and self-heal mat (optional)
- Steam iron

1. Open up the jumper into flat pieces by cutting along the side seams, around the armholes and across the shoulders. You will only need one piece of the main body for this project. The back of a jumper usually has more usable fabric than the front.

1

2. Place the flat jumper fabric piece sideways on a self-healing cutting mat. With extreme care, cut vertical slashes in the jumper, about 5-10cm/3-5in. long. You can use a metal ruler if you prefer, but make sure the blade can't slip onto your hand. The slashes need to run across the body not up and down – i.e., horizontal rather than vertical. If you prefer, you can mark the lines on with chalk or soap and use scissors to cut the slashes.

2

Felt the slashed jumper panel following the instructions on pp.37-8. Hang it up to dry and use an iron on medium heat with lots of steam to get all the creases out. The edges of the slashes will curl outwards. You can press them flat or leave them rolled, as you prefer. I have pressed them flat in these examples.

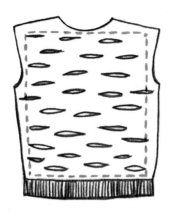

3

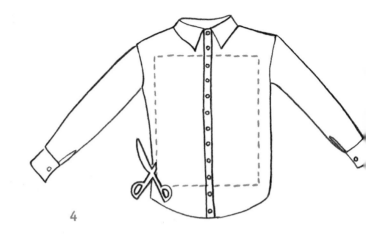

4

3. Place the slashed panel flat, close the slashed gaps and work out the size of cushion you can make from it, once you have cut off the cuff and ribbing on the bottom edge and straightened up the armhole sides. A large jumper should give you a rectangular panel about 40x25cm/ 16x10in., or you could make a smaller square cushion. Cut to the required size.

4. Open up the shirt in the same way as the jumper. Cut a panel the same size as your slashed felt panel from the front with the buttons in the middle and a matching piece from the back.

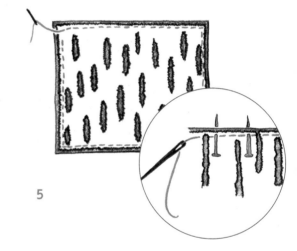

5

5. Use the plain piece from the shirt back as the backing fabric for the slashed felt. Pin the two pieces together all round the edges, closing up any gaps caused by slashes on the edge. Tack in place by hand and remove the pins. Undo some of the middle buttons on the shirt panel, then place it button-side down on top of the lined felt panel, which should be right-side up. Pin in place and machine sew all round the cushion with 1.5cm/⅝in. seam allowance. Remove any buttons in the seam allowance. Remove the tacking, clip the corners (see p.67 step 5) and turn the cushion right way out. Press the edges.

7 Fashion projects

Shawl

I have a passion for colourful vintage ribbon and buy whole spools when I am lucky enough to find it. This shawl is a great showcase for some special ribbon. The basic embellished panel of fabric can be made into an unlined wrap, a shrug or a doubled-sided shawl as desired. You may wish to use a smaller piece of fabric to make a scarf or a larger piece for a shawl/wrap.

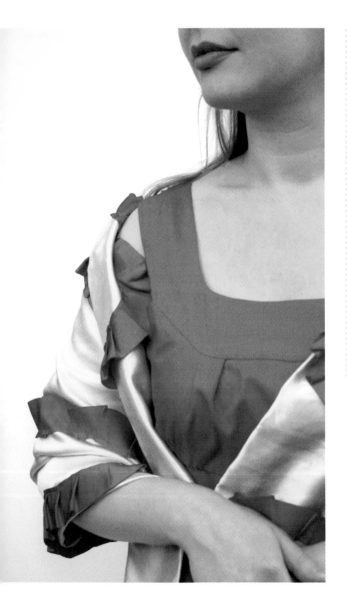

Materials

- 80cm/31in. of fabric at least 145cm/60in. wide
- 6-10m/2$\frac{1}{2}$-4 yards. of 2.5cm/1in.-wide ribbon (err on the side of caution and start with more rather than less!)
- Matching sewing thread. If machine sewing, you may want to use a bobbin thread which matches the fabric and a top thread which matches the ribbon. If hand sewing just use a thread which matches the ribbon.

Equipment

- Hand sewing kit
- Machine sewing kit

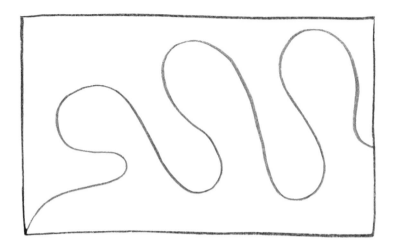

1

1. Spread the fabric out on a table, right side up. Use a vanishing pen, soap or chalk to mark a gently curving line snaking across the fabric. Start the ribbon at one edge of the fabric and have a couple of centimetres overlapping the edge.

2. Pleat the ribbon into gentle curves and make small pleats (about 1cm/½in.) in the ribbon, about 5-10cm/2-4in. apart. Put a pin in each pleat. Make sure all the pleats fold in the same direction.

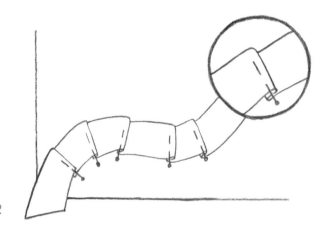

2

3. When all the ribbon is pinned in place, machine sew along one side of the ribbon, a few millimetres (¼in.) from the edge, making sure you are sewing in the same direction as the pleats. Remove the pins as you come to them. You can also sew down the other side if you wish, starting at the same end to avoid puckering the ribbon.

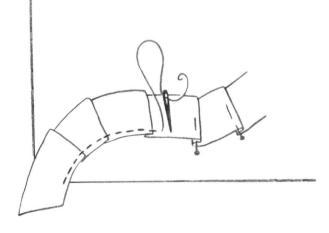

3

Once the embellishing is complete, you need to choose what you want to do next.

a. You can simply hem the edges and use as a wrap. You could sew in a lining in the same way as in the scarf project on p.104.

b. Make a shrug by hemming the short ends, then turning the rectangle inside out and sewing the long seam leaving a gap of about 50-60cm/20-24in. in the middle. Turn under the raw edges and slip stitch in place.

c. Make a double-sided shawl as shown. Fold the embellished fabric right sides together and sew the long seam leaving a 15cm/6in. gap in the middle. Open it out and place the seam facing up in the centre. Sew across the short ends. Turn out through the gap, push out the corners with a knitting needle and slip stitch the opening closed.

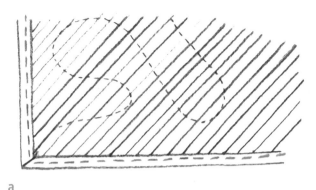

a

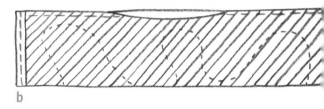

b

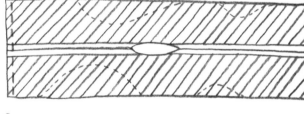

c

Scarf

The lines of corduroy, laid in different directions, inspired this design, which looks like a pinwheel. It would also work well in a striped fabric like a recycled pinstripe shirt. You might like to use a plain or contrasting backing fabric; a patterned vintage fabric would look fantastic, or you could make two sets of pinwheel panels and have a double-sided scarf.

Materials
- 1m/1 yard organic cotton corduroy (at least 100cm/1 yard wide)
- 1 large size men's shirt or 100cm/1 yard organic cotton or other medium-weight fabric (any width)

Equipment
- Hand sewing kit
- Machine sewing kit

1. Cut eight 17cm/7in. squares on the straight grain. Cut four of the squares diagonally in half with the ridges running downwards and cut the other four squares in half diagonally with the ridges running across.

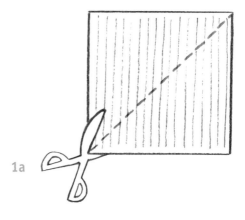

1a

1b

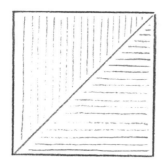

2

3

2. Pair up triangles from each pile so each set creates the lines as shown when the diagonal cut edges are put together.

3. Sew each pair of triangles together, being careful not to stretch the fabric as you sew along the bias. Press the seam allowances open then trim off the excess.

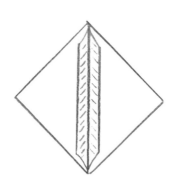

4

4. Trim the seam allowances (see p.60) and cut off a little at each end as shown.

5. Arrange two squares in the formation shown, then put right sides together, making sure the diagonal lines match and sew together along the centre seam. Trim the seam allowances as before. This makes half of the pinwheel panel.

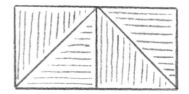

5

6. Sew another pair together and place one above the other as shown, ensuring that they are placed correctly and that the lines match neatly. Sew together as before. Repeat to make the second panel. Trim the edges so both panels are completely square. This makes the pinwheel panels.

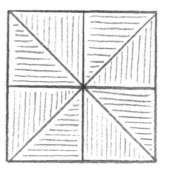

6

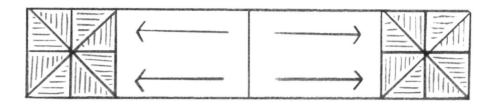

7

7. Cut two pieces of corduroy each 65x25cm/25½x10in. Ensure the corduroy pile runs downwards on each piece and sew the pinwheel panel to the ends. Trim the seam allowance. Join the two pieces together and press all the seam allowances open.

8. Make the backing panel by cutting 25cm/10in.-wide strips from the shirt – you should get two from the back and need just one front to make a piece about 130cm/51in. long. Sew all the pieces together (making sure the seams are all on the same side) and press the seam allowances open. Place the corduroy scarf piece face up and the lining face down on top of it. Pin in place and sew all around,

8

leaving 20cm/8in. open at one side. Trim the seam allowance all the way around, except across the opening. Clip the corners (see Step 5 on p.67). Turn the scarf the right way out, push out the corners with a knitting needle and press all the edges flat. Fold under the seam allowances in the opening and sew up by hand using slip stitch (p.58).

Lace bag

I have a huge stash of vintage lace, which I never know what to do with, so I designed this bag to make use of these wonderful motifs. Peace silk in natural creamy-beige colours perfectly complements the old lace

Materials

- ½m/20in. peace silk (two different weaves a&b, or both the same) or medium-heavy weight vintage or recycled fabric, any width
- ½m/20in. organic cotton or other lightweight lining fabric, any width
- Vintage lace motifs
- 1m/40in. string

Equipment

- Pattern pieces p.113
- Hand sewing kit
- Machine sewing kit

Pattern pieces can be found on p.113. Enlarge 250% and cut the following:

- *Front pocket piece*- cut one from peace silk (a) and one from organic cotton for the lining.
- *Main pattern piece*- cut two from peace silk (b) and two from lining fabric.
- *Handles*- from lining fabric, cut two strips each 65cm/26in. x 7cm/3in.
- *Inner pocket*- from lining fabric, cut one piece 12cm/5in. x 10cm/4in. or what-ever size you prefer.

NB: 1.5cm seam allowances are included in the pattern pieces and the measurements given in the instructions.

1. Position the lace motifs on the front pocket panel. Sew on using small stitches all around the edges, making sure you do not pucker the fabric.

2. Place the front pocket piece with the lace face up, and the pocket lining piece face down. Pin in place and sew around the

1

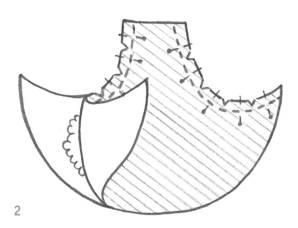

2

curved pocket openings. Trim and clip the seam allowances (see p.60).

3. Turn the pocket piece the right way around and press the pocket edges. Sew around the edges of the pockets with small running stitch (see p.57) about 5mm/½in. from the edge, to stop the lining from curling out and to make the pocket opening neat.

4. Place the front part of the main bag fabric (peace silk b) face up and position the pocket piece face up on top. Pin in place all around. Mark the centre line with chalk and machine sew along the centre. This creates two pockets and stops the pocket from sagging. Tack across the top part, through all layers. Place the front piece face up and place the back piece (peace silk b) face down on top. Pin around the edges and sew the curved seam, through all layers. Trim the seam allowances by about half their width. Clip the curves (see p.60).

5. Make the handles. Fold the strips in half lengthways, with the right side in. Press lightly. Take a length of string about 80cm/31in. long and tie a knot in one end. Place the string inside the folded strip, so the knot pokes out at one end. Sew across the short end, catching in the string, and along the side of the strip. Pull the end of the string and work the tube inside out. Cut off the sewn end and remove the string. Press the tube flat, with the seam along one edge. Repeat with other handle.

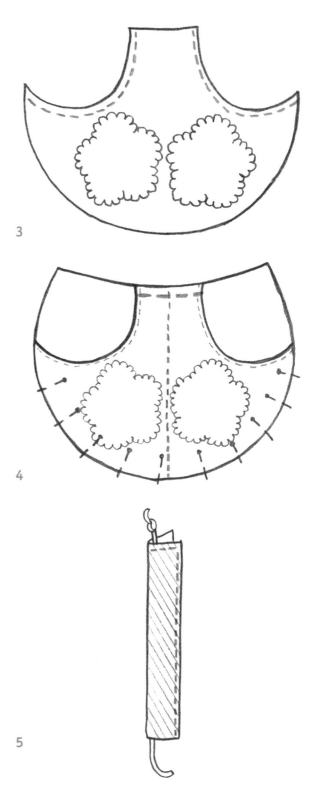

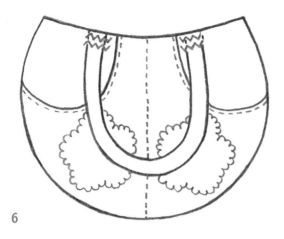

6

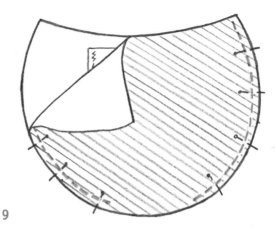

9

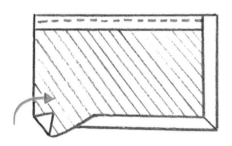

7

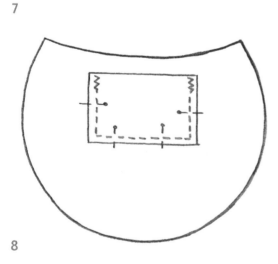

8

6. Position the first handle on the front of the bag as shown. Sew zigzag stitches very close to the edge to hold the handles in place then go over the same stitches again. Sew the other handle onto the back of the bag, matching the position of the front handle. When you sew the lining to the bag the zigzag stitching is hidden.

7. Make the inner pocket. Turn over one long edge and press under. Sew across. Then fold under the seam allowances on the other edges and press in place. Fold the corners neatly.

8. Sew the pocket to the right side of one piece of the lining. Position it in the centre then sew along one side, across the bottom and up the other side. Start and end the stitching with some zigzag stitching to stop the top of the pocket from tearing.

9. Sew the front lining to the back lining by placing right sides together (pocket inside) and sewing around the curved edge. Leave a gap as shown on the pattern piece. Trim the seam allowances (see p.60), except across the gap.

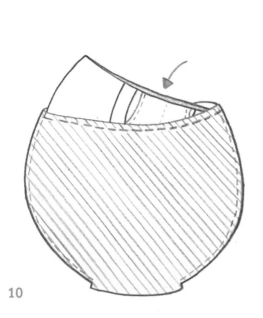

10

11

10. Leave the lining inside out and place over the top of the main bag, making sure the handles are tucked inside. Make sure the side seams match. Sew around the top of the bag, through all the layers. The zigzag stitching holding the handles on should be inside the seam allowance. Trim the seam allowance.

11. Turn the bag the right way out through the gap in the lining. Sew up the gap in the lining by hand using slip stitch (see p.58). Press the top edge of the bag and top stitch in the same way as the pockets in step 3. Remove the tacking thread.

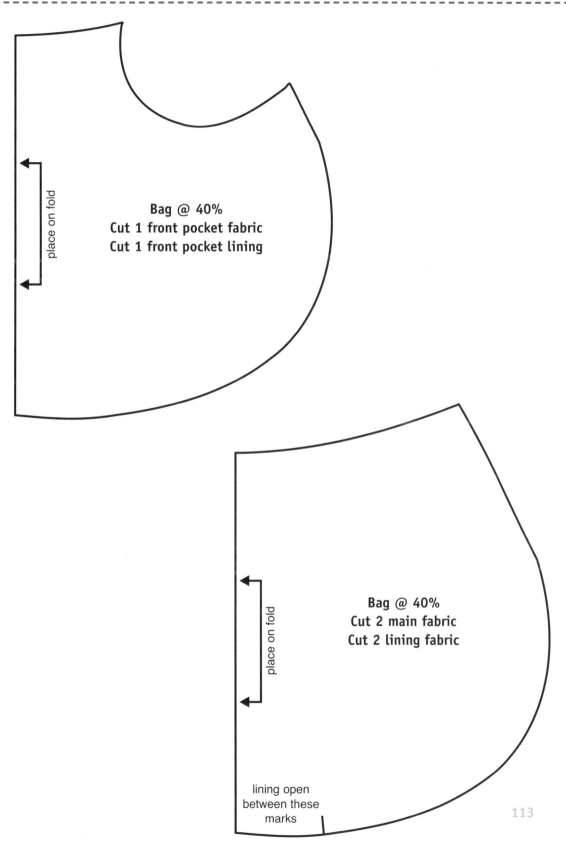

place on fold

**Bag @ 40%
Cut 1 front pocket fabric
Cut 1 front pocket lining**

place on fold

**Bag @ 40%
Cut 2 main fabric
Cut 2 lining fabric**

lining open
between these
marks

113

Purse

This small zip purse is ideal as a pencil case or make-up bag. It is best made from a fairly sturdy fabric that will hold its shape. You can enlarge the pattern to make a bigger purse if you wish – just substitute a longer zip.

Materials

- 25cm/10in. of any width of fabric or 35x35cm/14x14in.-piece medium-weight cotton fabric such as Harmony Arts Organic Cotton
- Scrap of wool felt
- One 28cm/11in. zip (if you need to shorten the zip see p.61)

Equipment

- Machine sewing kit
- Purse pattern piece* on p.117. Enlarge the pattern by 200% on a photocopier
- Leaf template on p.117

*1.5cm/⅝in. seam allowances are included in the pattern piece.

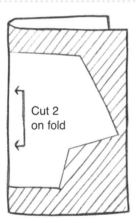

Cut 2
on fold

1

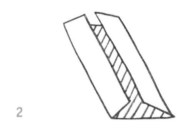

2

1. Cut two panels using the pattern piece. Place the side of the pattern marked with an arrow on to the folded edge of the fabric.

2. Cut two tabs each 4x4cm/1½x1½in. Fold the edges to the middle and press.

3. Position the tabs on the front purse piece, 1.5cm/⅝in. in from the end, with the raw edges facing up. Tack in place.

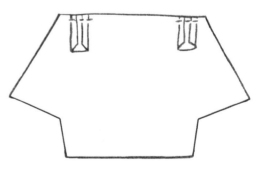

3

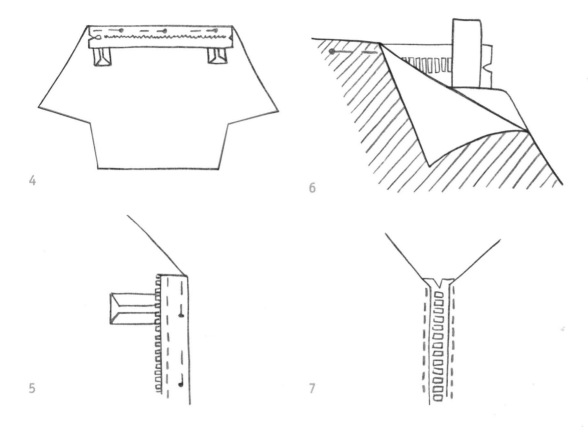

4

5

6

7

4. Place the zip FACE DOWN on the purse front with the ends on the tabs. Unzip part way down.

5. Starting at the open end of the zip, sew along, close to the teeth, using a zip foot (see p.62). When you reach the zip pull-tag, leave the needle in the fabric, lift the presser foot up and slide the zip-pull back to the top. Put the foot back down and continue sewing.

6. Fold the purse front down so the zip lies face up. Position the purse back piece so the raw edge matches up with the top edge of the zip, with the tab sticking up. Pin in place. Turn over and sew along the zip tape,

as close to the teeth as possible, with the zip uppermost. Move the zip pull-tag along as before.

7. With the purse and zip the right way up, fold the fabric so the fold is close to the zip teeth and sew again, close to the fold. This covers up most of the zip tape and gives a neater finish. You can skip this step if you prefer.

8. Open the zip halfway. Fold the purse in half, so the right sides of the fabric are facing each other. Match the corners and pin in place. Fold the zip in half and pin. Sew across the folded zip slowly and carefully (as the zip teeth can break the

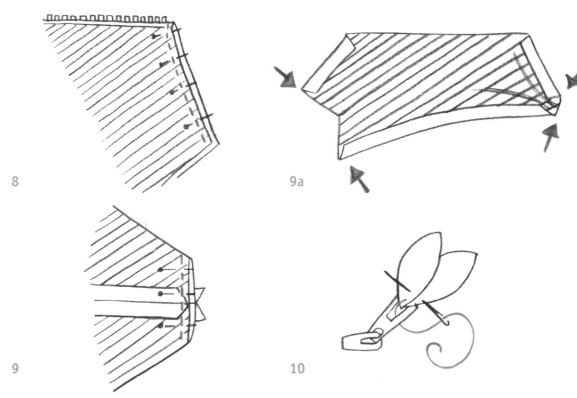

8

9a

9

10

needle) and along the side of the purse. Repeat for the other side. Then sew along the bottom.

9. Open the zip halfway. Press the seam allowances open near the open corners. To make the boxed corners, you need to sew the gap closed. This is confusing, so pin and tack first, then turn out the purse to make sure it is right before you sew. Instead of sewing straight down the seam, you need to fold the opening so the two seams come together, face to face, making the purse 3D instead of flat. Hold the seams and bring them together. Then sew across the corner, keeping both seam allowances flat. Turn the right way out and press the corners.

10. Cut two leaves from recycled felt using the template. Hand-sew onto the zip pull-tag using a double thread.

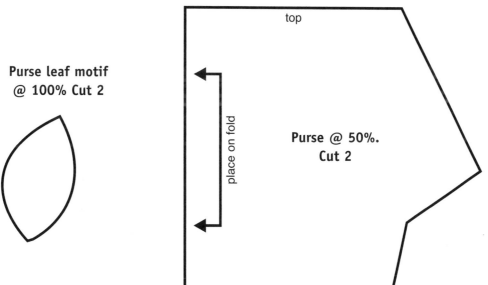

**Purse leaf motif
@ 100% Cut 2**

top

place on fold

**Purse @ 50%.
Cut 2**

Cuff

This frivolous and frilly cuff really dresses up an outfit. You can make a matching pair or just wear one as a bracelet. You could even sew them onto the cuffs of a jacket or top.

Materials
- Fabrics as below
- 40cm/16in. of narrow ribbon (about 5mm/½in. wide)

Equipment
- Hand sewing kit
- Machine sewing kit

You will need to cut bias-cut strips of fabric following these instructions. Fold the square of fabric in half diagonally and iron the crease. Unfold then cut along the crease. Measure the width of the strip required from the crease and cut strips as required. It is best if you can cut the strips in one piece rather than joining them together as this will hinder the gathering. A 40cm/16in. square of fabric will give you a diagonal strip length of 50cm/20in. with plenty to spare.

Cut the following:
- 3 strips of different fabrics, each 50cm/20in. long:
  - One 8cm/3in. wide (bottom layer fabric)
  - One 6cm/2in. wide (middle layer)
  - One 3cm/1½in. wide (top layer).

Because you cut the fabric on the bias (diagonal) it doesn't fray or curl. Very loose-weave fabrics will fray a bit, so choose something with a tight weave (no gaps between the threads) and quite firm.

Medium-weight cotton, silk or stiff synthetics work well, rather than floppy velvet or chiffon. Vintage shot taffeta works very well. If you want to use organic fabrics, choose firm-weave cotton or hemp rather than a loose weave peace-silk. The main fabric (8cm/3in. strip) needs to be fairly stiff but the upper fabric can be soft and floppy. If you are unsure, try a test piece and see how it works.

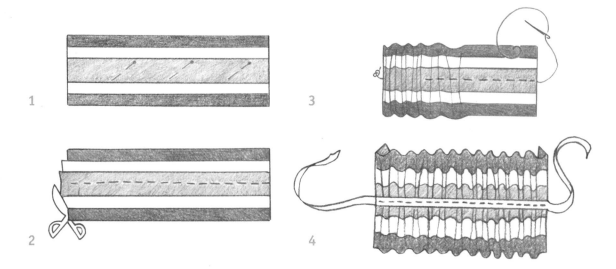

1. Layer the three strips with the widest at the bottom and the narrowest on top, with the right sides of the fabric facing up and the ends matching.

2. Pin together then machine- or hand-tack down the middle to hold all the layers together. Some of the layers might stretch a little, so trim the ends so they are neat.

3. Using a double thread with a strong knot, start sewing from the underside and make running stitches along the middle of the cuff, following the previous line of sewing. The stitches should be medium-large, about 7-8mm/¼-⅓in. long. Don't fasten off the thread at the end, leave the

needle attached and pull up the thread to create gathers. Pull up, and slide the gathers down until the cuff is about 20cm/8in. long. Using the same needle, make a couple of small stitches on the back of the cuff to fasten the gathers in place. Cut the thread. Remove the first tacking thread (not the gathering thread!).

4. Fold under each end of the cuff by about 5mm/¼in. and pin in place. Position the ribbon centrally on the cuff and pin in place. Machine- or hand-sew along the middle of the ribbon, making sure you catch in the folded under-ends of the cuff. Fasten the thread firmly at start and end by reversing.

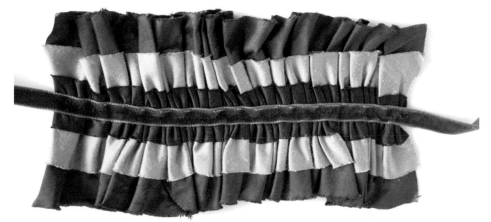

Embellished coat

I love embellished, embroidered winter coats but they are usually beyond my budget. I designed this project as an excuse to revitalise an attractive but ordinary coat and turn it into something spectacular. I've used thin leather in a rather amazing silver colour – scraps from a costume designer! Use any fine leather scraps or recycle a suede or leather skirt (as used in the cushion on p.85). If leather doesn't appeal or isn't available then you could use recycled wool felt, as in the pincushion project on p.64. Use the iron-on template method as described. You could also use a combination of leather, felt and embroidery; appliqué would be an excellent way to embellish the hem, cuffs or collar instead, or as well as, the centre front.

Materials
- Leather/suede or felt scraps
- Old coat
- Card for template

Equipment
- Hand sewing kit
- Hand sewing leather needle (these have a triangular tip and will go through the leather much more easily than a normal sewing needle)
- Polyester thread (leather can rot cotton thread)
- Ballpoint or felt-tip pen
- Template below

Coat before

Motif for coat @ 100%

1

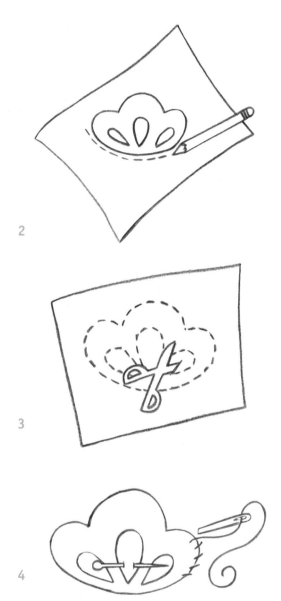

2

3

4

1. Draw out and trace your chosen design onto scraps of paper and pin onto the coat to decide upon the arrangement. Or use the template on p.120 and add motifs down the centre front as I have.

2. Make a cardboard template of the design and draw around it onto the back of the leather using a ball point pen or felt tip. If the leather is dark, try a soft pencil and work in natural daylight.

3. Cut out the leather shape using sharp scissors. To cut the holes, make a small snip within the hole and use small scissors to cut out.

4. If you use shapes with holes in them, you can pin through the holes to hold the pieces in place. Don't pin through the leather as any holes you make will be permanent. You could also hold the appliqués in place temporarily with a few dots of fabric glue.

5. Sew using polyester thread and a leather needle, using small slip stitches (see p.58). Bring the needle up through the fabric and leather, about 2-3mm/⅛in. in from the edge and then sew back down through the fabric, bringing the needle back up into the leather to make the next stitch.

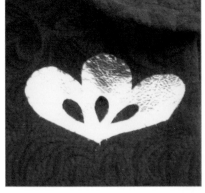

Detail of leather appliqué

The finished coat

Corsage

I designed this corsage specifically to use leather samples I was given by an interior designer. To get leather scraps you could try leather furniture outlets for their old colour sample packs, any furniture maker who uses leather, shoe-makers and bag-makers.

Materials
- A small piece of medium-weight leather which is easy to cut with scissors
- A small amount of firm felt
- Vintage or other button at least 1.5cm/⅝in. diameter
- Safety pin
- Fabric glue

Equipment
- Hand sewing kit
- Template below

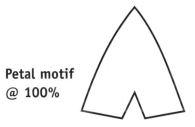

Petal motif @ 100%

1. Cut two circles of felt, each 4.5cm/1¾in. diameter. On one circle, mark an inner circle 1cm/½in. from the edge (soap slivers work well for marking felt). Draw around the template using ballpoint pen or felt tip on the REVERSE side of the leather. Cut 13 petals. Apply a small amount of glue to the reverse side lower edge of each petal, either side of the V. Leave to dry for a few minutes until clear and tacky.

1

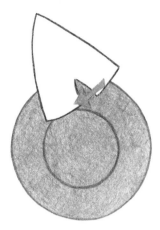

2

3

4

2. Apply the first petal by pressing down one side of the V to the marked inner line, then bringing the second side up close, so the V is closed and the petal curls upwards. Hold firmly for a few seconds until stuck.

3. Continue with seven more petals, overlapping them slightly each time.

4. Repeat in the same way for the inner circle, making sure you leave a small hole in the middle to sew on a button. Leave to dry then choose a button large enough to cover the edges of the inner circle of petals. Sew through the felt.

5

6

5. Sew a safety pin onto the other piece of felt, making sure you sew the closed side down, so it will still open.

6. Sew the pinned-circle to the edges of the brooch circle, around the outer edge.

Hat

A few years ago, wide-brimmed floppy felt hats were all the rage and now you can find them in charity shops.

Materials

- One wide-brimmed hat. If you can't get a hat with a wide brim, use a second felt hat to cut up. Cut it open and use a steam iron to press the pieces flat. You could use felt from one hat to decorate a straw or fabric hat too.

Equipment

- Hand sewing kit
- Steam iron
- Slivers of soap to mark the felt. These will disappear when you steam the felt.

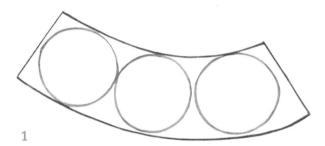

1

2

3

1. Take off any hat trimmings and mark a cutting line on the brim by measuring 3cm/1½in. out from the hatband line so there is a small brim remaining. The remaining hat brim will be used to make the decorations. Find a suitable circle template (jar or pot about 6-7cm/2⅓-3in.) the same width as the felt scrap. Draw around the circle template using soap and cut out as many circles as you can.

2. On each circle, cut a line to the centre.

3. Twist the cut circle into shape. Pin it to the ironing board then hold a hot steam iron over it. Hover the iron, press the steam button and hold for a few seconds. Leave the circle to cool completely. You can pin and steam all the circles in one go. Once the twists are cool, they should hold their shape.

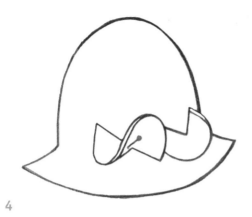

4

5

4. Arrange the twisted circles as desired on the hat, pinning in place, straight through.

5. Sew on by hand using a few small stitches on either side of the fold.

6. If you have any felt left over, use two circles to make a brooch. Leave one circle uncut then cut, twist and steam the other as in Step 3 on previous page. Sew the twist onto the plain circle and sew a safety pin or brooch pin on the back.

Hat before

Curtain skirt

Vintage curtain fabrics make wonderful skirts. This simple pattern makes the most of bold printed fabrics and is quick and easy to make – it takes about two hours to sew.

Materials

- One curtain big enough to fit the pattern pieces or approx 1.5m/59in. other fabric
- One 15cm/6in. zip
- Hook and eye
- Safety pins
- 10cm/4in. of medium-weight fabric at least 85cm/34in. wide or piece strips together to make a piece long enough for the waistband
  Cut a waistband 5cm/2in. wide and the length required for your size:
  Size 10: 73cm (29in.)
  Size 12: 77cm (30½in.)
  Size 14: 81cm (32in.)
  Size 16: 84cm (33in.)

Equipment

- Hand sewing kit
- Machine sewing kit

- Skirt pattern pieces on p.132. The pattern includes UK sizes 10, 12, 14 and 16 and includes 1.5cm/⅝in. seam allowances. **Please note** US sizes are different, roughly two sizes smaller, so a UK 14 is a US 10. Enlarge by 300% on a photocopier and stick pieces together to make full-size pattern pieces*. This should work with two pieces of A3 paper, or go to a copy shop to have it printed out on one piece of large paper.

*Double check the size before you cut the fabric! The straight seam should be 63cm/24⅘in. long. The finished length is 23in. or 58cm. Check another skirt to establish if this is too short for your height and add extra length to the hem if you need to.

Read the general information about recycling curtains on p.34 before you start this project.

1. Untie the curtain pleating tape and unpick it. Unpick the hems if you will need all the fabric. Wash and press the curtain. Mark any stains or damage with safety pins. Fold lengthwise, with the pattern on the inside, making sure it is straight. Enlarge and cut out the pattern piece for your size.

For the front of the skirt, place the pattern piece with the straight seam on the fold and draw around it. Ignore the notch on the straight seam.

= wrong side of fabric

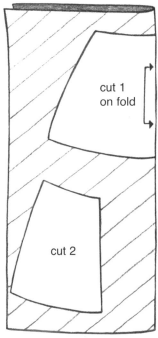

cut 1
on fold

cut 2

1

To cut out the back piece, position the pattern piece on the same alignment (so the pattern runs in the same direction) and make sure the grain line (long arrow marked on the pattern) matches the direction of the vertical threads in the fabric. Try to avoid any of the marked stains. Draw around the pattern piece and mark the zip placement notch (on the straight seam) and the side-matching notch on the curved seam.

If you need to cut the fabric out in one layer, place the front pattern piece on the fabric, draw around it, then flip it over carefully, matching up the edges, and draw round it again. You can do the same with the back piece, but make sure you flip it over so you get a right piece and a left piece!

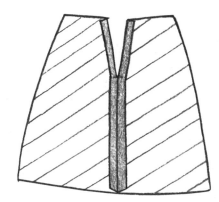

2

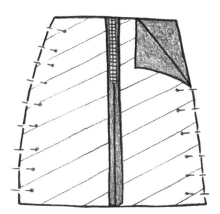

3

2. If the fabric frays a lot, zigzag all the edges before you start sewing up. Sew up the back seam as far as the zip placement mark. Insert the zip following the instructions on p.61.

3. Place the skirt front piece face up. Place the skirt back piece (with zip) on top, face down, making sure the matching up marks are correctly positioned. Pin, then sew the side seams.

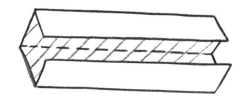

4

4. Cut a waistband from the same fabric or a contrasting one, to the size given above. Fold the waistband in half lengthways, with the right sides facing. Press lightly. Unfold, then press one long edge to the centre, then the other. Unfold one edge.

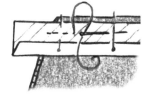

5

5. Pin the unfolded edge to the waist of the skirt, with 1.5cm/⅝in. overlapping at the starting edge. There should be 2.5cm/1in. overlapping at the other end. Sew along the crease.

6. Press the waistband up from the front.

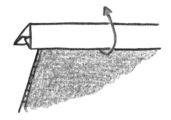

6

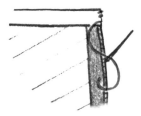 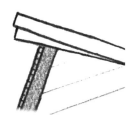 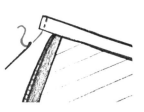

7   8   9

7. Press the waistband over onto the back, making sure the raw edge is folded under. Tuck under the short end of the waistband and stitch in place.

8. At the long tab end of the waistband, fold the waistband in half, with the right sides together, so the folds match.

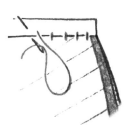

10

9. Sew across, 1.5cm/⅝in. in from the end. Turn the waistband right-side out and push out the corner with a knitting needle.

10. Hand sew the waistband to the skirt, making sure your stitches are small and neat, so they don't show through on the right side.

11

11. Sew on a hook and eye.

12. Try on the skirt and adjust the hem if it is too long or uneven. Take it off again then fold up a 2cm/1in. hem all round, pressing as you go. If it refuses to lie flat, make tiny pleats in the hem and then press into place. Sew by hand or by machine.

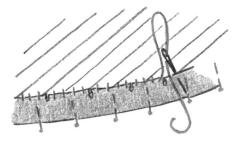

12

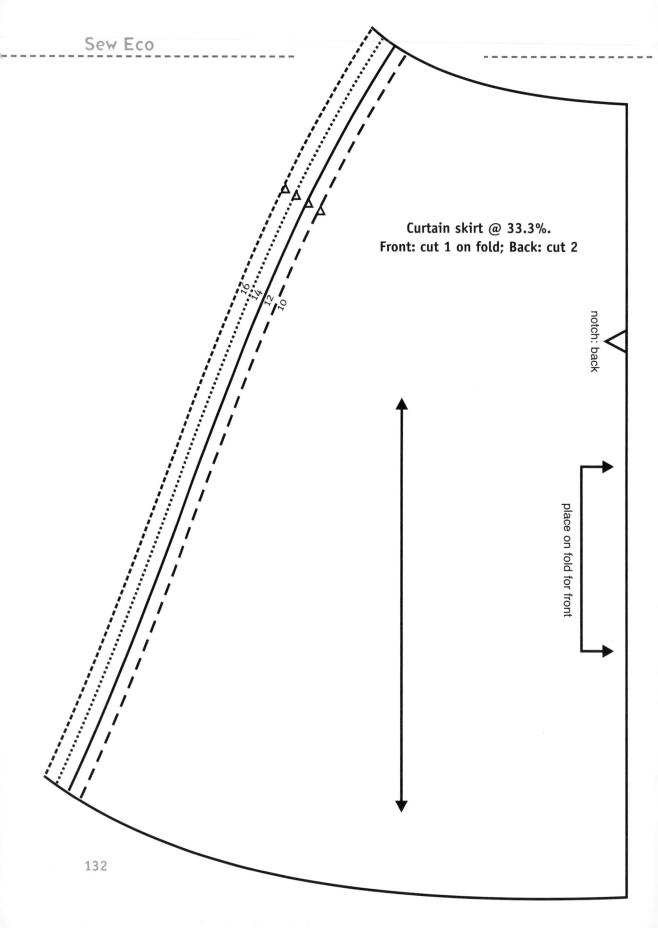

Curtain skirt @ 33.3%.
Front: cut 1 on fold; Back: cut 2

16
14
12
10

notch: back

place on fold for front

Blossom skirt

Re-vamp a plain skirt into a work of art using just scraps of fabric. The skirt I used is plain, lightweight cotton. Any skirt of any length could be used, but an a-line shape works well. Choose a selection of four or five co-ordinating colours to make the blossoms, or just stick with one colour.

Materials

- A skirt
- Scraps of fabric

Equipment

- Circle templates (tubs, jars, old CDs)
- Hand sewing kit
- Hanger, dressmakers' dummy or friend

Blossom skirt before

1

2

1. Cut about 50 circles ranging in size from 8-11cm/3-4in. Cutting each one individually takes ages, so cut three or four rough squares of fabric big enough for each circle template and make them into a pile. Pin together, then draw around the template on the top layer only, using a fabric pen or pencil. Cut through all layers.

2. Group the circles together in sets of about three (depending on how thick the fabrics are), making sure the right sides face up. The fabric on the top layer is the one that will show the most.

3. Fold each group of circles in half, then in quarters. Using a matching thread, stitch the circles together, hiding the knots inside the folds. Keep the stitches small and neat and just stitch through the point, not down the sides.

4. When all the blossoms are made, hang the skirt on a hanger or mannequin and pin the blossoms on to the skirt. Make sure you don't pin into the lining, if the skirt has one. I have arranged the blossoms around the side seam and slightly to the front, spreading out towards the hem. When you are happy with the arrangement, sew the blossoms in place, just at the points, so they can still move around a little. Be careful not to pucker the skirt as you sew them on, and only use a few stitches at the very tip of the blossom to attach them.

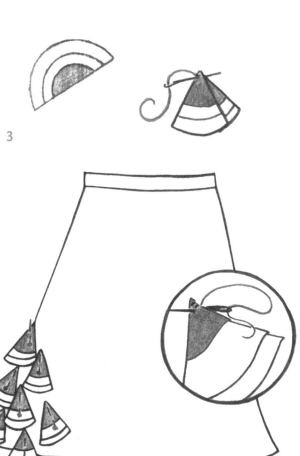

3

4

'Blossom' details

Conclusion

Sewing eco may seem too small an activity to make an impact on the world, but every little action has an impact. Even just making a small change in the way you shop and sew will make a difference. Your choices filter down to those you make for, those you share with and those you inspire – they too can take on the message of sewing eco and treading lighter on the earth either in the fabrics they use, or the clothes they buy.

Even if you only change one thing, make the most of that one change and share it. Don't feel guilty about those changes you haven't yet made, it is not always easy. The choices out there can sometimes seem just too numerous, so start local, keep it simple and follow your heart. Sewing is a joy and a pleasure – don't let eco guilt dry up your creative flow! We must accept that we can't always have everything we want, and learn to embrace what we do have and enjoy it fully. Of course the new fabrics in the shops will look tempting, but you should remember how wonderfully interesting, original and full of history vintage fabrics can be. Celebrate your sense of achievement in creating something new and fresh from something old and tired. Enjoy discovering the new eco fabrics that are increasingly available. Your positive choices make the world a better place.

Second to the activity of sewing itself, the thing I love most about being a textile designer is the chance to share my love of sewing with so many people. I've taught hundreds of people over the years and always enjoyed seeing the spark of inspiration and excitement as they discover a new way of working with fabric. Writing books allows me to share my love of sewing with so many more people. I hope this book really does inspire you to break new, green ground and make wonderful things. Don't forget to share your skills, whether by making presents for those you love or by teaching a new-found skill to a friend so you can share the pleasure and spread the message of eco sewing and green living. Sharing with other people is what matters most. Change the world, one stitch at a time.

Glossary

Bamboo: Fabric or yarn made from cellulose from the bamboo plant.

Barkcloth: A crinkle-weave fabric, usually cotton. Popular in the 1950s.

Biodegradable: A material which decomposes in the ground.

Buckram: A stiffened hessian fabric used for pelmets.

Burn-out: See *devoré*.

Calico: In the UK calico is a cheap, unbleached cotton fabric. In the US it is usually a printed lightweight cotton.

Cashmere: Yarn and cloth made from the wool of the Kashmir goat. Very lightweight and very warm.

Cellulose: Fibre produced by chemically-extracting polymer from a plant material. See also *bamboo*, *viscose*, *rayon* and *PLA* (*Lyocell*).

Chintz: Cotton fabric with a shiny, glazed (with special treatment) surface. Commonly used to refer to printed floral fabric, but chintz traditionally refers to the glazed surface.

Colourfast: A fabric dyed with a colour that will not run in the wash.

Cotton: Fabric or yarn produced from the cotton plant.

Crêpe: A fabric woven with very tightly spun fibres which give the fabric a slightly rough texture. Usually wool or silk.

Devoré: A type of patterned fabric where the design is in raised velvet or satin with a sheer background. A chemical is applied which burns away part of the velvet pile or satin surface. Also called *burn-out*.

Dupion(ni): A type of silk, often woven by hand, with small slubs or lumps on the yarn. Sometimes called raw silk. Shantung is similar, but lighter. Not the same as *wild* or *peace silk*.

Felt: Non-woven fabric made by compacting fibres. Traditionally made of wool or animal fibres, craft felt is usually synthetic.

Flannel: Brushed cotton or wool fabric with a fluffy surface.

Flax: The plant which produces linen.

Fleece: Either the shorn wool of a sheep or other animal, or a warm, fluffy cloth created from polyester, also called polar fleece.

Grosgrain: A ribbon or fabric woven with a ridged effect.

Hemp: Yarn and cloth made from the fibres of the hemp plant.

Horsehair: A type of stiff braid or fabric made from horsehair used to shape hems or garments.

Ingeo: Trademarked name for *PLA fibre*.

Interfacing: A special fabric used to support or stiffen the main fabric in garments.

Interlining: A fabric used for stiffening, supporting or adding opaqueness or warmth between outer fabric and lining fabric.

Jersey: A knitted fabric, such as T-shirt or sweatshirt material, often cotton. Sometimes includes Lycra.

Lawn: A fine, tightly-woven cotton cloth, either plain or printed. Often a good quality, lightweight fabric.

Linen: Yarn and fabric produced from the flax plant.

Lyocell: New cellulose-based fibre mainly made from eucalyptus. Trade name *Tencel*.

Lycra: Brand name for a synthetic yarn which can stretch many times its length. Included in many mixed fabrics for resilience and stretch. Called *Spandex* in US.

Merino: Very soft wool from the merino sheep (often Australian).

Microfibre: Extremely fine synthetic yarns which are often silky in feel.

Mohair: Yarn and cloth made from the spun hair of the angora goat.

Muslin: In the UK this is a cheap, loose-weave cotton fabric. In the US it means a *toile*.

Nylon: Synthetic fibre made from oil.

Organza: Silk or synthetic woven fabric which is transparent and slightly stiff. Silk organza is used for pressing cloths as well as fine clothing.

Peace Silk: Silk made from silkworms that have been allowed to complete their natural life cycle. Sometimes called *wild silk*.

PLA: Polylactic Acid, a new type of plant-based polymer which can be made into fibre. Usually made from corn.

Polyester: Synthetic fibre made from oil.

Ramie: A yarn and cloth made from plant fibre, similar to linen or hemp.

Rayon: An early manufactured cellulose fibre, made from wood pulp. Was used as synthetic silk commonly from the 1930s.

Satin: A type of weave, with a smooth surface on the right side, produced by a diagonal (*twill*) weave.

Shantung: See *dupion*.

Silk: Fabric or yarn produced from the cocoons of silkworms.

Spandex: US trade name for *Lycra*.

Tencel: See *Lyocell*.

Taffeta: A crisp, plain weave fabric, traditionally silk, now usually synthetic. It is stiff and has a characteristic rustle when worn.

Toile: A garment made to test the fit using a cheap fabric.

Tweed: Usually a wool fabric, medium-heavy weight used for coats. Often has flecks of other colours in the yarn. Traditionally used for coats and jackets.

Twill: A weave structure which gives a diagonal effect on the right side. Satin and denim are twill weaves.

Velvet: Fabric which has been woven with a pile, or raised surface. Can also be made from knitted (jersey) fabric and can be cotton, silk or synthetic.

Viscose: A type of cellulose fibre.

Worsted: A yarn and fabric made from lustrous and hard wearing types of wool.

Wadding: Thick layer of stuffing used for quilts. Can be polyester, wool, cotton or silk, or new fibres.

Wild Silk: See *peace silk*.

Stockists

For a full up to date listing of suppliers, please see: www.seweco.co.uk

UK Suppliers

Organic, sustainable & fair trade fabrics

Organic Cotton Fabrics Ltd.
www.organiccotton.biz
Fair-trade organic cottons in a wide range of colours
Machynlleth,Powys SY20 8DG

Greenfibres
www.greenfibres.com
Suppliers of organic and sustainable fabrics, stuffing and other materials
0845 330 3440

Bishopston Trading
www.bishopstontrading.co.uk
Fairtrade organic fabrics and clothing
0117 924 5598

Hemp Fabric UK
www.hempfabric.co.uk
Organic hemp and other fabrics
01271 314812

Fair Trade Fabrics
www.fairtradefabric.co.uk
Organic, fair trade cotton by the metre or in fat quarters for quilters
0845 1161893

Majestic Textiles
Suppliers of organic silk fabrics
No certification shown
www.organicsilks.co.uk
020 8808 2458

Ian Mankin Fabrics
Organic cotton/linen ticking and other organic cotton fabric
www.ianmankin.co.uk
020 7722 0997

Draper's Organic
www.drapersorganiccotton.co.uk
08452 60 35 60

Gossypium
www.gossypium.co.uk
Small range of organic, fairtrade fabrics as used in their own products
0870 850 9953

The Hemp Shop
www.thehempshop.co.uk
Suppliers of hemp fabrics
0845 123 5869

Harlands Organic Furnishings
www.organic-furnishings.co.uk
Specialist suppliers of organic fabrics, mainly for soft furnishings

Well Cultivated
www.wellcultivated.co.uk
Wide range of bamboo fabrics

Cloth House
47 & 98 Berwick Street, London
www.clothhouse.com
020 7437 5155
Limited range of organic cotton and other fabrics, plus English wool and pure wool felt by the metre

Absolution Saves
www.absolutionsaves.com
Will print to commission on organic fabrics with non-toxic dyes

M is for Make
www.misformake.co.uk
UK retailer for Cloud 9 printed organic cotton made in the US

Ardalanish Isle of Mull Weavers
www.ardalanish.com
Organic wool tweed made in Scotland
01681 700265

British Made Eco
www.britishmadeeco.co.uk
Organic and sustainable fabrics

Sukie
www.sukie.co.uk
Small range of organic cotton printed fabrics

K1 Yarns
www.k1yarns.co.uk
Limited range of organic cotton printed in Scotland
0131 226 7472

Denise Bird Woven Textiles
Ethical and organic textiles
www.denisebirdwoven
textiles.com
info@denisebirdwoventextiles.com

The African Fabric Shop
www.africanfabric.co.uk
Not officially Fairtrade status but
ethically-sourced fabrics
01484 850188

Myriad Online
www.myriadonline.co.uk
100% wool felt including
natural-dyed and organic
stuffing wool

Handmade Presents
www.handmadepresents.co.uk
Wool and organic wool felt
including naturally-dyed

Twisted Thread
www.twistedthread.com
Organisers of Festival of Quilts
and Knitting & Stitching Shows
where a range of independent
fabric suppliers can be found.

The Original Re-enactors Market
www.reenactorsmarket.co.uk
Market for historical re-
enactment. Suppliers of wool
and linen fabrics from various
sources

Naturtuche
www.naturtuche.de
German supplier of historical
fabrics including some naturally-
dyed wool and hemp fabrics

Local materials

Ask in your local shop for British
wool fabric and Irish linen

Curlew Weavers
Troed-yr-Aur Old Rectory,
Rhydlewis, Newcastle Emlyn,
Ceredigion
01239 851357
Welsh-made wool fabrics

Harris Tweed
www.harris-tweed.co.uk
Tweed fabric produced in
Scotland using wool from a
variety of sources

Givans
www.givans.co.uk
Irish Linen

Wingham Wool Work
www.winghamwoolwork.co.uk
Yarn, wool tops and wool stuffing

Historical Management Associates
www.stuart-hmaltd.com
historical_fabrics.php
Reproduction historical fabrics
made from wool and other fibres

Abimelech
www.abimelech.co.uk
Wool fabrics woven in Yorkshire
0113 395 5678

British Wool Marketing board
www.britishwool.org.uk

www.masseyandrogers.co.uk
www.stjudes.co.uk
Hand-printed fabrics made in the
UK

Volga Linen
Russian and European linen
fabrics
www.volgalinen.co.uk
0844 499 1609

The Linen Shop
Fabrics woven in Europe
www.thelinenshop.biz
01403 891073

Melin Tregwynt
Welsh-wool upholstery fabrics
www.melintregwynt.co.uk
01348 891 644

Natural Dyes

The Mulberry Dyer
www.mulberrydyer.co.uk
Naturally-dyed wool embroidery
threads and dyestuffs
01824 703616

Fibrecrafts
www.fibrecrafts.com
Supplier of natural dyestuffs
01483 565800

Renaissance Dyeing
www.renaissancedyeing.com
Natural dyestuffs, yarns and
threads
(France) 0033 (0)561 052760

Other

Green Earth Dry Cleaning
www.alexreid.co.uk/greenearth

The Laundry
www.starchsupplies.co.uk
Natural starch

Scrap Store Directory
www.childrensscrapstore.co.uk

Nichols Buttons
www.nicholsbuttons.co.uk
Collectible vintage buttons

Cotton Patch
www.cottonpatch.co.uk
Wool, cotton, recycled polyester
and silk quilt wadding

World of Wool
www.worldofwool.co.uk
Wool stuffing (non-organic)

Folksy
www.folksy.com
Online shop for indie craft
makers and suppliers in the UK

Ecopell
www.schomisch.de/us/1_ecopell.
htm
Producers of vegetable tanned
leather (Germany)

A W Midgley and Sons
www.awmidgley.co.uk
01934 741741
Vegetable tanned leather

Cameron Gilmartin
Digital printing
www.camerongilmartin.co.uk

Woad Inc.
Natural dyeing with woad.
www.woad-inc.co.uk

Fibre Harvest
Processors of UK-sourced fibres
www.fibreharvest.co.uk

Vintage Fabrics

Rag Rescue
www.ragrescue.co.uk
Vintage fabrics and trimmings;
mainly small pieces for
patchwork

Classic Modern
www.classic-modern.co.uk
Vintage 50s-70s furnishing
fabrics

Blankits
Recycled wool blankets
www.blankits.net

Donna Flower
www.donnaflower.com
Vintage fabrics and haberdashery

Vintage Fabric Market
www.vintagefabricmarket.co.uk
Vintage fabrics mainly in small
pieces for patchwork

Ebay UK
Ebay.co.uk

P&A Fairs
www.pa-antiques.co.uk
Organisers of Vintage Fashion
Fairs and London Antique
Textiles, Vintage Costumes &
Tribal Art Fair

The Textile Society
www.textilesociety.org.uk
Organisers of the Antique Textile
Fair

Anita's Vintage Fashion Fairs
www.vintagefashionfairs.com

*The Affordable Vintage Fashion
Fair*
www.vintagefair.co.uk

Other (Non-UK) Suppliers

Mountain Mist EcoCraft
www.mountainmistlp.com/
ecocraft.htm
Producer of Ingeo-based stuffing
and wadding
Available from
www.fabricshack.com.

Near Sea Naturals
www.nearseanaturals.com
US online store selling a wide
range of organic fabrics and
haberdashery including organic
cotton ribbon and sewing thread

Umbrella Prints
www.umbrellaprints.bigcartel.com
Hand-printed organic fabrics
from Australia

Harmony Art
www.harmonyart.com
Organic printed fabrics
Available in the UK from
Harlands Organic Furnishings
(see above)

Daisy Janie
www.daisyjanie.com
Organic printed fabrics. US.

Betz White
www.betzwhite.com
Organic printed fabrics. US.

Mod Green Pod
modgreenpod.com
High-end designer organic
furnishing fabrics. US.
Available in the UK from
Harlands Organic Furnishings
(see above)

Feltorama
www.feltorama.com
Wool and recycled polyester craft
felt. US.

Spoonflower
www.spoonflower.com
Digital printing of your own
design onto fabric, including
organic cotton. US.

Resources

Ethical fashion, research and design

Black, S. *Eco-chic: The Fashion Paradox*. Black Dog Publishing, 2008.

Fletcher, K. *Sustainable Fashion and Textiles: Design Journeys*. Earthscan, 2008.

Fashioning an Ethical Industry
http://fashioninganethicalindustry.org

Ethical Fashion Forum
www.ethicalfashionforum.com

Labour Behind The Label
www.labourbehindthelabel.org

Ever and Again Research into Upcycling Fashion and textiles www.everandagain.info

Textiles Environment Design www.tedresearch.net

Textile Future Research Unit www.tfrg.org.uk

Sustainable Manufacturing Group, Cambridge University. Download a copy of *Well dressed? The present and future sustainability of clothing and textiles in the United Kingdom* www.ifm.eng.cam.ac.uk/sustainability

Information on eco textiles

www.organic-furnishings.co.uk

www.treehugger.com

http://organicclothing.blogs.com

Nature Works LLC. Producers of Ingeo (PLA) www.natureworksllc.com

Also see fabric suppliers for information on their products.

Organisations

European Textiles Network
www.etn-net.org

Oeko-Tex testing for harmful substances in textiles www.oeko-tex.com

Soil Association for organic certification in UK www.soilassociation.org

Pesticide Action Network www.pan-uk.org

WRAP UK Government run waste recycling programme www.wrap.org.uk

Environmental Justice Foundation cotton research www.ejfoundation.org/page141.html

Fair Trade Foundation www.fairtrade.org.uk

British Wool Marketing board
www.britishwool.org.uk

Australian Wool Innovation www.wool.com.au

Anti-mulesing campaign www.savethesheep.com

Craft & Sewing

www.seweco.co.uk

www.mantua-maker.blogspot.com

http://whipup.net/

www.sewgreen.blogspot.com

www.burdastyle.com

www.wardroberefashion.net

http://craftingagreenworld.com

www.threadbanger.com

Singer, R. *Sew It Up. A Modern Manual of Practical and Decorative Sewing*. Kyle Cathie, 2008

Singer, R. *The Sewing Bible*. Potter Craft, 2009

Balfour-Paul, J. *Indigo*. Archetype Publications Ltd, 2006

Blaydes, C & Smith, N. *Fashion DIY. 30 Ways to Craft Your Own Style*. Sixth and Spring Books, 2007

Chanin, N. *Alabama Stitch Book: Projects and Stories Celebrating Hand-Sewing, Quilting and Embroidery for Contemporary Sustainable Style*. STC Craft/A Melanie Fallick Book, 2008

Flint, I. Eco Colour: *Environmentally Sustainable Dyes*. Murdoch Books, 2008

Karol, A. *Bend the Rules Sewing*. Potter Craft, 2007

Ganderton, L. *Vintage Fabric Style*. Ryland, Peters & Small, 2003

Gridley, J S; Kipling, J R; McClure, J S. *Vintage Fabrics Identification and Value Guide*. Collector Books, 2006

Mornu, N. (Ed). *A is for Apron: 25 Fresh & Flirty Designs*. Lark Books, 2008

Mullin, W. & Hartman, E. *Sew U Home Stretch*. Little, Brown & Company, 2008

Mullin, W. & Hartman, E. *Sew U: The Built by Wendy Guide to Making Your Own Wardrobe*. Little, Brown & Company, 2007

Ordoonez, M. *Your Vintage Keepsake: A Csa Guide to Costume Storage and Display*. Tech University Press, 2001

Prideaux, V. T*he Handbook of Indigo Dyeing*. Search Press, 2003

Rudkin, L. *Natural Dyes*. A&C Black, 2007

White, B. *Sewing Green. 25 Projects Made with Repurposed & Organic Materials*. Stewart, Tabori & Chang, 2009

White, B. *Felt So Good: Over 30 Irresistibly Cute, Cosy and Colourful Felted Projects*. David and Charles, 2008

Willoughby, A. *49 1/2 Skirts*, A&C Black, 2008

Magazines

Selvedge www.selvedge.org

Threads www.taunton.com/threads

Craft www.craftzine.com

Index